Welcome to Paranor⌐

It was important for me to develop Paranormal Perspectives for those seeking a deeper understanding of the paranormal world. This series is intended for sceptics, believers, and those who have unfathomable experiences and are often frightened by them. These books will help their understanding of what is happening to them.

The Paranormal Perspectives series will explore, in-depth, the encounters, theories, and research into incomprehensible events and how these experiences motivated remarkable individuals to delve deeper and share their extraordinary relationships of the paranormal with the world.

Paranormal Perspectives begins with five books exploring the spectrum of metaphysical events, with insight from the UK's top ghost detective, a licensed clinical psychologist, a retired English professor, a prolific UFO investigator, and a writer specialising in first-hand, personal paranormal encounters.

You, too, may have had a lifetime of unearthly experiences and may wish to add to the series. Please visit 6th-books.com for further information. We look forward to hearing from you.

I hope you enjoy this series as it guides you on your quest and pulls back the veil to shine light into the unknown.

Sleep well,

G L Davies

Author of *Haunted: Horror of Haverfordwest*

Paranormal Perspectives

One Big Box of 'Paranormal Tricks': From Ghosts to Poltergeists to the Theory of Just One Paranormal Power
by John Fraser

A Jungian Understanding of Transcendent Experiences
by Susan Plunket

Hauntings, Attachments and Ghouls
by G L Davies

Portraits of Alien Encounters Revisited
by Nigel Harry Watson

Where the Spirit Led
by Brad Burkholder

What People Are Saying About

Paranormal Perpsectives
One Big Box of 'Paranormal Tricks'?

John's book whirls through his experiences and hypotheses investigating this fascinating topic touching on subjects such as the ethics involved, hypnotic regression, poltergeist phenomena and good old fashioned paranormal research.

From his earlier days at university right up until how this book was written, John explains how investigating the paranormal is never a straightforward path with his accounts filled with balance and often providing a thought — and yet allowing the reader to make up their own mind.

This book is like opening John's mind and having a chance to poke about, ultimately understanding what makes this man tick, all the while sprinkled with the Fraser humour throughout. He's certainly an individual we shall be reading about in many years to come.

Beth Darlington, Director of Access Paranormal Website, Paranormal Journalist/Podcaster

John takes us on a journey through an ordinary life which has been enchanted by following the spirit of a scientific and enquiring mind. Stepping outside of the mainstream, mundane world John has discovered himself wandering along the avenues of our world which journey into a 'paranormal life' towards the possibility of a paranormal theory of everything.

Along the way, we learn of his encounters with some of ghost hunting's great names. We discover some of the investigations he has been involved in, and his knowledgeable use of measuring equipment, both old and new. He reveals his Sherlockian approach to investigating, which helps eliminate possible everyday causes when pursuing the causes of alleged paranormal phenomena. John shows the importance of knowing not just the background history of places and persons involved in cases, but also the limitations of the equipment used in investigations. The importance of being alert to the pastoral implications of performing investigations, no matter what may appear to be happening at a location appears throughout.

Matt Arnold, Editor of *The Christian Parapsychologist Journal*, Paranormal Researcher/Writer.

Paranormal Perspectives: One Big Box of 'Paranormal Tricks'?

From Ghosts to Poltergeists to the Theory of Just One Paranormal Power

Previous Books by the Author

Ghost Hunting: A Survivor's Guide (2010). Cheltenham: History Press. ISBN-10: 9780752454146

Poltergeist! A New Investigation into Destructive Haunting: Including 'The Cage — Witches Prison' St Osyth (2020). Winchester/Washington:6th Books. ISBN-10: 1789043972

Paranormal Perspectives: One Big Box of 'Paranormal Tricks'?

From Ghosts to Poltergeists to the Theory of Just One Paranormal Power

John Fraser

6TH
BOOKS

London, UK
Washington, DC, USA

CollectiveInk

First published by Sixth Books, 2024
Sixth Books is an imprint of Collective Ink Ltd.,
Unit 11, Shepperton House, 89 Shepperton Road, London, N1 3DF
office@collectiveinkbooks.com
www.collectiveinkbooks.com
www.6th-books.com

For distributor details and how to order please visit the 'Ordering' section on our website.

Text copyright: John Fraser 2023

ISBN: 978 1 80341 524 6
978 1 80341 532 1 (ebook)
Library of Congress Control Number: 2023933919

A CIP catalogue record for this book is available from the British Library.

Design: Lapiz Digital Services

UK: Printed and bound by CPI Group (UK) Ltd, Croydon, CR0 4YY
Printed in North America by CPI GPS partners

We operate a distinctive and ethical publishing philosophy in all areas of our business, from our global network of authors to production and worldwide distribution.

Contents

The Supernatural is the Natural, just not yet understood.

Elbert Hubbard

A world in which there are monsters, and ghosts, and things that want to steal your heart is a world in which there are angels, and dreams and a world in which there is hope.

Neil Gaiman

(Authors Note: Two quotes are unusual to sum up a book. They are necessary in this case; necessary to feed the fascinating different desires of the logical left side of our minds and its constructive conflict with its mischievous impulsive romantically intuitive right side. Whilst it is possible the brain's intuitive right side may hold the key to paranormal powers, this book is a tribute to both parts of the brain as it is the balance that makes us human.)

Preface

What Makes a 'Good' Paranormal Perspective?

There are different ways of investigating that which is currently regarded as being 'occult' or 'paranormal'. On the extremes, there are those who investigate to re-validate what they already know is true. There are also those who investigate to 'ridicule' what they already know to be false. For both of these extremes there is nothing, in effect, to investigate. Their purpose seems only to reinforce their perspective of life on others.

In many ways this is the norm in our lives — people like to deal with certainties. Sometimes only such certainties send a clear message to the reader and the listener, and for that matter the church goer as well. Even bona fide paranormal researchers can tend to send out a message of certainty.

Harry Price, perhaps the best-known paranormal researcher in the twentieth century, is a good example of this. His famous study of Borley Rectory, published in 1940, was called *The Most Haunted House in England*, without the hint of a question mark in the title! More recently, in 1980, my former colleague Guy Playfair titled his study of the famous Enfield Poltergeist *This House Is Haunted!* Perhaps eager readers would prefer to hear that certainty when compared with the more thoughtful invented title *Is the Enfield House Really Haunted?*

Such certainties can have their dangers when dealing with real life paranormal type incidents. This is especially so when dealing with people under stress because of strange inexplicable events, who are told with 'certainty' that these incidents are caused by a restless spirit, or far worse, a demonic 'portal' to hell. Whatever your inner beliefs, if you wish to have a 'good' paranormal perspective do not go around calling yourself a

'Demonologist' or similar name, a mistake that is commonly made. Most prominent of those who have made such a 'mistake' would perhaps have been the self-proclaimed 'Demonologists' Ed Warren and his wife, Lorraine. The Warrens became famous for investigating the Amityville Horror case as well as other places that have also been made(in)famous in the 'inspired by true events' popular series of movies known as *The Conjuring*.

Gerald Brittle, in his book, *The Demonologist*, a biography about the Warrens, quotes Lorraine Warren as saying:

> Only the demonic, however, [as opposed to an earthbound human spirit] has the power to bring about negative phenomena as fires, explosions, dematerialisations, teleportation, and levitation of large objects.
> (The Demonologist, p. 17)

This is, perhaps, a Christian fundamentalist good versus evil view of the paranormal. For the sake of my point, let's put aside its likely truth or otherwise. My point being that if this was the very first thing that a family heard from experts during a poltergeist case, such certainty would do the opposite of reassure. It would be nearly guaranteed to exacerbate the mental trauma. In the Enfield case, mentioned above, Janet, one of the young girls, who appeared to trigger the phenomena, was reported to have levitated. Imagine the impact on a young girl if she was told without doubt, as per Lorraine Warren's quote, that levitation meant she was under the control of a 'Demon'?

The 'Occult' is often defined as the study of mystical, supernatural, or magical powers. Whilst this definition is correct, both the Occult and the Paranormal have an underlying and perhaps a more useful meaning as well. The Oxford Online Dictionary gives an interesting example of its use to convey the concealment or hiding of one celestial body from another: 'The Moon occults Mars during daylight on March 22.'

This shows, in effect, that 'Occult' can simply mean 'hidden'. For the purpose of our journey, it's most neutral meaning is simply powers that are currently hidden from our normal understanding of science. Likewise, what else can 'paranormal' mean without, in effect, becoming 'normal' and fully explained? There should be no presuppositions at first as to what that hidden knowledge could possibly be.

Certainty in such a subject is surely only in the domain of fools, or of those unduly influenced by others, or of those who wish to self-proclaim as a cult-like 'godhead'. I hope you will see in the forthcoming chapters that I make no claim to be a 'godhead'! I also take full account of the influences that others have had on me (especially in Chapter Two). As for being a fool or otherwise, I will let the reader decide.

I feel the acknowledgement that the paranormal is uncertain, elusive, and sometimes very tricky to prove (or disprove) is what turns people into effective researchers of the subject. It is what, in effect, makes a 'good' paranormal perspective. This is, of course, my own subjective 'good' as I would not wish to fall into the same 'absolutist' trap that I believe the Warrens and others, including 'devout' disbelievers, fall into.

After all, if religion can be a powerful influence in the belief of what the paranormal might be — equally so is a 'religious' disbelief of religion. If we are looking for book titles that sum up that philosophy, in my opinion look no further than *The God Delusion* (2006) by philosopher Richard Dawkins. This book title sums up the equally 'fundamentalist' view taken by some when a subject (be it God or the paranormal) is outside their own fixed beliefs. Going back to the Enfield example, would the Hodgson family have appreciated (in the middle of objects flying around their house) a Dawkins type mentality that simply politely lectured them that all such events were 'metaphysically impossible' — that they were simply under delusion? I am not quite sure such words of wisdom would have had the desired calming effect.

A good perspective, I think, should be to approach our subject in an open, sceptical, but empathetic way. Not afraid to question but not afraid to acknowledge that our own material understanding of the world as yet may not hold all the answers. It never has in the past since the time of Alcmaeon of Croton c. 500 BC. (Who despite being hailed by many as the father of anatomical science still concluded that goats breathed through their ears.) Why then should fixed 'scientific' theories of 'delusion' be the final word for such strange unexplained and such worldwide phenomena?

A good paranormal perspective must also include the ability to dream and want to experience the impossible, be it through a slightly surreal 'road trip', which you will read about in Chapter One, to more practical efforts that you will read of in later chapters. The 'impossible' is after all a cunningly flexible concept. A few will still remember pre-1954 proclamations that a four-minute mile was impossible until Roger Bannister dared to dream and achieve.

Finally, a good paranormal perspective must accept that whilst science is not the same as truth, it is an important process. A process that will help our understandings of things not yet fully understood. We should also remember that science often works best with one big overriding theory explaining a lot of phenomena — could it possibly be the same when it comes to phenomena currently termed as paranormal?

Lots of 'tricks' but, in effect, one big paranormal box?
John Fraser, Croydon, Surrey, UK
jfraserparanormal@yahoo.com

Acknowledgements

For the writing of such a book the acknowledgements may seem few but, in effect, Chapter Two is an acknowledgement to those who helped me on my paranormal quest.

Over and above those mentioned in that chapter, I would like to give a special thanks to:

Dr Robert Radaković (PhD) for his general support and for his intriguing thesis on the genesis of psychical research (which helped bring me to some conclusions in Chapter 8), as well as organising interesting speakers on the subject which helped clarify my thoughts.

Also, to:
Dr Urszula Wolski (MSc) and **Claire Davy** for being two of those very interesting speakers whose talks helped inspire those thoughts.

Chapter 1

In the Beginning
(Every journey needs a starting point)

In the beginning I think we are all born with curiosity for the unknown. Even from the young infant who has just protothoughts, (primitive sensory and emotional ones) without the language to be self-conscious, still eagerly reaches out to directly experience the new feel of a smooth or a rough surface; to experience something which is cool, something that is warm and something that is sometimes far too hot! That instinctive response of a high-pitched cry bringing the 'pioneering explorer' back to the familiar comfort of his or her mother's arms.

I clearly remember when just slightly older, spending what seemed like hours tracing my fingers along the line that goes round a tennis ball. I remember my growing fascination that the lines connected with each other and took my finger on an endless journey. It was perhaps my first experience of the concept of infinity. A concept which while I accept today (and is fully accepted in mathematical models), I find still tricky to truly comprehend. A concept that a few centuries back could only be explained by adding your own personal or cultural 'god'.

Accepted knowledge, possible knowledge and impossible flights of fancy seem to be treated as an absolute by many, but they surely are related to the norms of a society and its level of understanding of the world. I was brought up on Apollo moon landings, and yet more Apollo moon landings till there were more Apollos than the younger children in my infants' school could count. Yet just a few generations before, the concept of live moving pictures let alone live moving pictures of men on the moon would have been scoffed at as 'paranormal' — the domain of dreamers, the domain of alchemists even the 'evil' domain of witches.

It also began to occur to me that with space apparently 'conquered', every highest peak of the earth climbed, and Jacques Cousteau plunging into the depths of the oceans at prime time on our new colour TV — what really was left for a young boy to explore? Were the truly 'inexplicable' goalkeeping skills of Peter 'The Cat' Bonetti, (an acrobatic shot saver who played for my favourite team, Chelsea) who I was to try for a time to emulate, as close as I was going to come to the true 'unexplained'? Even the fascination I had for those once mythological lizards known as dinosaurs had long been accepted by mainstream science.

I guess it's fair to say I was a 'highly inquisitive' child!

I mentioned earlier that belief and knowledge are to a large extent fed to us by the existing beliefs of our society. To the extent that this is true, it must also be true that the subcultures within each society — more commonly known as families, also have a very profound effect. Here perhaps I was lucky to achieve a good balance of a loving, open minded but largely sceptical father and mother. Both were to prove a valuable source of alternative explanations through the 'popular' waves of paranormal that the media proclaimed as inexplicable during the 1970s. The highlights of that period included the spoon bending and other talents of the very personable Uri Geller, whose 'talents' were to a large extent copied by the slightly less personable but renowned stage magician James Randi. Prominent in the media at that time was also an assortment of 'psychic surgeons' mainly from the Philippines and Brazil. Their 'talents', very different from that of traditional spirit healers, consisted of splitting a chest open and removing a tumour with their bare hands. This was marvelled at to begin with before being largely exposed as apparently fake. Whatever your belief in phenomena, I would hope that all would agree that a case of out and out fakery on the vulnerable should be against the morals of any culture. This in itself makes open minded scepticism vital.

As I grew up, I found myself becoming something of an intellectual disbeliever and yet still a dreamer who wanted to be wrong and wondered … *What if?* Perhaps a 'split personality' in this way is no bad thing for investigating things that are as yet 'unknown' and still far beyond our comfort zones of cultural belief?

But strangely, though, whilst we might reject the unknown and fear the unknown — secretly we all love the unknown or love to hate it at least!

What if bats could turn into caped blood sucking creatures?

What if dark shadows in ancient houses were timeless recordings of wicked black monks in hooded capes?

These are questions that have fascinated many, though, of that many, most only explore it through fiction. There is a near universal desire to 'love to hate' the unknown with either a book in their hands or from the safety of a cinema seat. In my case at that time this consisted of black and white horror films watched with my older sister long after 'official' bedtime had passed. I think we had perfected the phrase of 'Just ten more minutes please, Dad'.

We should not underestimate the power of fiction in opening the mind. However, knowing that something might actually be real takes that experience to a whole new level.

I think I was about 13 when purely by accident, I watched what was then very uncommon on TV. This was a rare documentary on 'real' ghosts long before the days when such things dominated the TV channels. A documentary called the 'Ghost Hunters' featured an investigator, Peter Underwood, and in particular featured the famous case of Borley Rectory and its ghostly nun who walked the grounds with a pained look on her face.

A case of solid facts sounding even stranger than that black and white fiction watched from the sofa. Also, a case that led to me emptying entire shelves from the local library on the 'factual paranormal' and tagging maps with every haunted place I could possibly find. I remember adding 'special tags' to cases of 'infamy' and those especially remote. I noted that those in less inhabited Scotland seemed more spine-chillingly 'romantic' than most. From recollection, I had no desire to investigate a haunted place where the noise of traffic obscures the noise of the ghosts. What would be the challenge when things got 'scary' if you could just jump on a bus and go home? The former point to this day remains valid and I have turned down investigations because of disturbance and noise pollution that makes getting to the truth a near impossible task. The latter point is intellectually invalid but still holds to this day a certain 'romantic' appeal.

I think at this time in my adolescence my ambitions of being the next Peter Bonetti were also put to one side. Apart from paranormal distractions, my rate of growth had slowed, and I was never going to reach the 6ft-plus height required to be successful at a high level as a goalkeeper.

My first attempts at paranormal investigation at the age of about 14 were amusing and somewhat silly. If we are being honest, most things we do at 14 normally are! There was a plan to ghost hunt at the George and Dragon, a famous haunted pub in West Wycombe, Buckinghamshire, to which I still had enough alternative kudos to persuade a group of friends of mine to arrange to join me on. The venture was never to go ahead though as one by one my friends' parents stopped them from going. They likely sensibly realised that a bunch of male juveniles couldn't get into a pub let alone make any attempt to investigate it for the presence of ghosts. A misreading of the telephone directory would have put paid to these plans in any case. The pub we were meant to have been heading to was in fact the George and Dragon, West Wickham, Bromley, many miles away from its West Wycombe counterpart and its tragic tale of Suki, the maid, who died trying to meet her upper-class suitor in the nearby Hell Fire caves.

Of a far more practical and promising nature was the attempt I made the next year with a close school friend of mine called Jayesh. We had decided together to enter a television young filmmakers' competition, for which I persuaded him to agree to a documentary subject of haunting and ghosts. Now Jayesh, I believe, had no interest in the paranormal, but, as I was to discover, throughout his life, loved inspiring himself with new challenges. I assume that was why such a project captured his imagination and infectious enthusiasm. It also utilised his much better skills behind the lens than mine.

Our much more practical plans included places we could go to this time. We finally decided on a list of two. The first was Highgate Cemetery, thought to be the lair of a mysterious vampire. The second was the 'Silent Pool' in Shere, Surrey. This was thought to be haunted by a young lady who drowned when caught swimming naked by King John in the thirteenth century, and who swam too deep to avoid his unwanted attention.

In the late 1970s, mass ownership of video cameras was still at least a decade away and it was deemed acceptable to film in 'Super Eight' (old fashioned spool of film format) and add the recorded commentary separately to a cassette tape.

Our filming was quite professional, and we obtained interviews from friendly locals talking about vampire phenomena and overdubbed the rest. I honestly thought Jayesh and I had both done a very professional job and I had managed to obtain insights of how people respected the paranormal even when talking to a couple of teenagers. However, when the time came to edit and send in the entry, the taped commentary and more importantly the interviews had totally disappeared. All the possible tapes that could have contained them had 'mysteriously' been over recorded with editions of the top 30 pop charts. An accidental error where my family's liking for 1970s 'glam rock' ended a budding paranormal film career before it even had begun.

I think it was then that I learnt that paranormal investigating was full of strange surreal twists!

Though my interest in the paranormal never really stopped, it took a back seat for a while during my period of higher education. I studied Philosophy and Economics at Keele University; what I thought was a perfect balance for a dreamer and thinker and occasionally hard-headed sceptic. I also supplemented the desire to explore the more academic thoughts in my mind by writing poetry as well.

Philosophy is thought of by some as a whimsical subject but is a perfect way to train the mind to think. For example, I found myself questioning atheism. This was because science is fundamentally based around cause and effect. Yet as long ago as the time of the ancient Greeks, there was what has become the 'Unmoved Mover' argument raised initially by Aquinas. This basically states that if everything needed to be moved by a 'mover' or some other force, we sooner or later will ask the first question of who or what the first mover is. We either do this or engage in what seems like an absurd infinite regression of looking for further causes. This is a point that I feel Dawkins's *God Delusion* book (which I mentioned in the Preface) never seemed to cover. I was to find out later that I was not the only person at Keele to fully agree with that point.

This is no whimsical argument of abstract philosophy as the practical implications go very deep. Whilst there is clearly something missing without an 'Unmoved Mover', what is missing is clearly unlikely to be a dignified gentleman in robes and with a white beard. (This was a concept possibly first established as late at the fourteenth century by Italian artist Barnaba da Modena and reinforced by the Dutch Gothic artist Jean Malouel. Prior to this, 'God' was portrayed by a hand reaching down through the heavens, hence, from where the saying the 'Hand of God' emerged.)

What can be shown through that need for a first cause is a potential gap in our understanding of the world. This gap could be filled by a 'god' but could potentially also be filled by a 'paranormal box of tricks'. Something which is beyond our current understanding but less remote than that 'God' of Christian mysticism, and a power whose effects could at least have the potential to be greater understood. Whilst I have no orthodox religion, I was swayed, at that point, from 'atheist' to 'agnostic'. I could potentially be swayed much further if our understanding of apparently hidden powers becomes more complete.

I was a little disappointed as an undergraduate that my colleagues could in many cases get high marks for essays that just seemed to competently regurgitate established ideas from a textbook. This contracted with my more novel efforts (admitted, with bad handwriting and poor spelling) which seemed to get just adequate marks instead. There was one exception to this in the Philosophy department in the guise of a professor called Richard Swinburne.

I would perhaps in a complimentary way describe Swinburne as a pure academic — an incisive brain with a peripheral body attached. Swinburne had a lot to say on the necessity of a God to make our infinite Universe make sense. He was also sharp enough to absolutely insist that I open one of his tutorials, when the previous night I had spent too long in the student bar and was therefore ill prepared. No other student could start until I admitted my error which he accepted in good grace. This led me to believe that Richard Swinburne either had ESP powers, or he could read people so well that he would have been an excellent poker player in another life.

Swinburne's marks were never generous but always fair. He was to the best of my knowledge renowned for rarely if ever giving 'A' grades to students. I therefore considered it as high as the scale could go when once he gave me a B+ with a comment 'Or possibly better' within the margin. This was even more pleasing as the topic had fascinated me greatly. The topic was that of the philosopher Thomas Kuhn. It was about his then fairly recent revelations that the point of science was not to find absolute truth but simply the best working 'paradigm'. This gives the strange potential that the whole of science is wrong (or at least not absolutely right) in its underlying theories, even though the theories may to a great extent produce accurate predictions. More fuel to add to the fire that there may yet be something special still to discover.

I left university in 1985 towards the end of the greatest recession since the 1930s, three million-plus unemployed! I also noticed that every time the rate started to rise above this figure that the government under Margaret Thatcher would change the way the unemployment figures were counted. Politics, I then started to realise could be far less scientific than the paranormal. Under the Thatcherite slogan of 'There Is No Alternative' (to outmoded monetarist policies) industry shut and real 'ghost towns' started to flourish.

On a more practical point this also meant that most of the graduate jobs I applied for were politely rejected without an interview, and after several meaningless roles the one real opportunity that came my way was as an internal auditor at a large electricity company. This may have been fine for the practical left side of my brain but wholly unsuitable for the creative right side whose hope and dreams were reduced to audit tick boxes. The result was bouts of insomnia and quite severe panic attacks!

I remember, on a rather exhausting day off, watching the BAFTA award winning movie *Local Hero* (1983). This was about an American 'Yuppie' (a popular term then for 'young urban professional person in employment') being transferred to the desolate north of Scotland to buy land for an oil refinery. The American subsequently fell in love with the whimsical magic of the place.

Of this movie *The New York Times* Critic Janet Maslin was to write that it:

> Demonstrates ... [an] uncanny ability for making an audience sense that something magical is going on, even if that something isn't easily explained.

Perhaps it was something to do with the American in the movie feeling trapped like me and 'escaping', that made me fully agree with the critique of Ms Maslin. By the end of the movie I was uplifted and positive and mentally dusting down all the maps in which I marked those haunted places in remote Scottish locations nearly a decade before.

I also remembered back in high school reading the author Colin Wilson quoting Marcel Proust's *Remembrance of Things Past* (1913), and how Proust had had what Wilson described as a 'Peak Experience' — an opening of the mind both conducive to well-being and also possibly conducive to paranormal experiences.

Proust's experience revolved around the taste of a simple Madeleine cake bringing back the experiences he had in his youth and is so well written and uplifting it deserves a detailed quote:

> And soon, mechanically, weary after a dull day with the prospect of a depressing morrow, I raised to my lips a spoonful of the tea in which I had soaked a morsel of the cake. No sooner had the warm liquid, and the crumbs with it touched my palate, a shudder ran through my whole body, and I stopped, intent upon the extraordinary changes that were taking place. An exquisite pleasure had invaded

my senses, but individual, detached, with no suggestion of its origin. And at once the vicissitudes of life had become indifferent to me, its disasters innocuous, and its brevity illusory — this essence was not in me, it was myself. I had ceased now to feel mediocre, accidental, mortal.... How could I seize upon and define it?

In my case the way I tried to 'seize upon and define' the moment was to resign from my job and map out a route and plan to get to tip of the north-east of Scotland full of legends and haunting. I had one place in mind amongst others, a magical place known as Sandwood Bay complete with a desolate cottage whose only occupant was the ghost of a reputedly Polish shipwrecked sailor. This was also a place regularly written about by the paranormal investigator Peter Underwood whose documentary in the 1970s had started my strange interest.

The plan had practical elements of which my left brain should certainly take some credit. I had since become involved with international youth politics as International Officer of the Young Liberal Democrats, by part cunning planning and part coincidence a heavily subsidized international Youth Conference was taking place in April in the pretty town of Cupar in Scotland. This was about three quarters of the way to my destination which would not only pay for the petrol but give my ancient Vauxhall Viva a well-earned rest for a few days.

What could possibly go wrong?

No less than my gearbox irretrievably braking just on my arrival at the Cupar conference car park, with the age and condition of the car putting it past sensible economic repair!

With my chances of getting any further apparently negligible, I at least enjoyed the three-day conference with the camaraderie of likeminded young political people from all over Europe. For some strange reason that I can't quite remember, an impromptu football match was also held in which I inevitably played in goal. I (not always so inevitably) managed to keep a clean sheet for this makeshift international side of young politicians, some of whom were destined to follow their own dreams and head for much higher political office in time.

There was still, though, the little matter of the wreck of a car sitting in the parking lot. When it comes to the paranormal, however, be it experience or investigation, strange things often occur. No, the gearbox did not magically fix itself, but my practical left-hand mind had ensured fully comprehensive breakdown insurance cover. The insurance company was faced with an ultimatum to tow my car back 500 miles to London or to get the damned thing fixed! The next thing I knew I was at their regional centre being treated to coffee and biscuits. I was also listening to them frantically sourcing a second-hand gearbox that fitted my car on a Sunday, which by a small miracle they managed to do successfully from the few scrap yards that were open. Within a couple of hours I was driving out of the more densely populated parts of Scotland and into the magic of one of Europe's last true wildernesses.

But why Sandwood Bay?

I think the point I have been making over the last few pages is that every paranormal investigator needs both the credentials of an analytic thinker and the credentials of a 'What if...' romantic dreamer as well. Sandwood Cottage on the bay is so remote it is four miles off the nearest officially navigable road. It is also relatively close to the remote hotel at Kylesku, equally steeped in myths and legends of real or imagined ghosts. Particularly that of a man called Tordeas who had been pushed down the ladder in the hotel snuggery by his son, and who had since appeared on the spot. From talking to the staff I discovered the likely spot in question was just above the pool table at the hotel. Of course, I spent the night at the Kylesku Hotel though sadly I did not find a fellow traveller to engage in a game of pool with.

In some ways the whole thing was the ultimate road trip which made me feel like a modern-day Jack Kerouac, the US novelist and poet whose main work, *On the Road* (1957), founded the 'Road Trip' concept and the post-war beat generation. It was a very necessary road trip to start to get my head around the stuff of legends and understand the things that could be real and even ultimately later the things that could be faked. It was a road trip where I can still remember the things I ate and the feelings I got in the places where I stayed. It was a road trip where I felt 'invincible' enough the next day to drive my near wreck of a car a mile and a half off road confidently down the dirt track to Sandwood, without any fear it would let me down this time. A trip where I didn't check the weather which could have been bitterly cold in April in the far north of Scotland but which during my trip strangely stayed mild and clement.

It was perhaps during the overnight stay in the ruins of Sandwood Cottage where I got my sense of possibilities back. The only phenomena were quickly explained by the shine of an unseen lighthouse a few miles up the coast and the white silhouette of sheep on the horizon of the night. When the morning came, the cold meat pie I had for breakfast still tasted every bit as good as Proust's freshly baked Madeleine cake.

A full report is made of Sandwood in my earlier book *Ghost Hunting: A Survivor's Guide* (2010); the main points of which are based on the research I did interviewing the locals and in Glasgow Central Library a few days later. I discovered that:

Many of the reports of a ghost came second-hand from one source, a local author of folklore, R. MacDonald Robertson. Whilst I have little doubt that Robertson took these reports in good faith, they are clearly taken at face value without the questioning mind that any paranormal researcher must have. An example of this is that one main witness, a shepherd called Sandy Gunn, is also reported by Robertson as seeing a mermaid as well. This was apparently noted by Robertson without further comment or question. For reasons such as this, I now find that the key to good paranormal research is to vet the original source of reports and unwind the likely truth.

Whilst Sandwood Cottage was indeed uninhabited, nearby there was an equally remote bothy (cottage) which had for years been inhabited by quite a famous recluse by the name of James McRory Smith. McRory Smith's striking appearance matched that of archetypical 'bearded sailor' perfectly. These could potentially explain the later sightings that were mainly reported directly to the author and researcher Peter Underwood. For those who want to judge for themselves, I would recommend the website jamescarron.wordpress.com/features/surviving-strathchailleach.

McRory Smith was a fascinating man by all accounts but it's just possible that he may have unnerved some brave campers at Sandwood Cottage or Bay. Particularly, if by chance he was seen staggering about in the twilight, after a glass or two of his favourite 'High Commissioner' brand of fine scotch whiskey.

If we assume, for argument's sake, that the sailor did exist as a paranormal entity, there was little evidence for his Polish nationality which was likely added as an embellishment over the years. The Polish theory is of particular interest for two very good reasons.

The first of these being that any paranormal investigator must be aware that such embellishments happen. We must not accept witness testimony without a polite bit of ethical probing of the facts. Our task is very different from that of R. MacDonald Robertson who, as a folklorist, had simply the task of recording traditional beliefs, myths, tales, and practices. This is fascinating, but paranormal investigators also have the responsibility to get to the truth of the matter.

For the second reason, we should take a small leap of faith and assume the gentleman spirit was in fact Polish. Yet we still find one well recorded sighting in 1949 involving the sailor telling two men to 'leave his property' quite clearly speaking in English. We can debate the possibilities of an ancient foreign mariner being able to speak English or not. However, the more interesting point of debate is that direct paranormal communication rarely, if ever, comes in a way the receiver cannot understand. This is of particular interest when it comes to other communicatory type phenomena, of which more will be said later in this book.

So, the jury is very much out on this strange case of the phantom bearded sailor but there are some interesting postscripts to this equally strange road trip.

A few years later, the dirt track was closed off to ensure anyone venturing to the bay did indeed have a four-mile walk. More importantly, at some point the roof mysteriously vanished from the cottage and ensured this 'romantic' road trip could never be done in quite the same way again.

I corresponded with Peter Underwood and was asked to join the then 'exclusive — by invitation only Ghost Club' of which he was President at that time. I also used the report to become an accredited investigator of a new and vibrant organisation: the Association for the Scientific Study of Anomalous Phenomena (ASSAP).

Just over a decade later, with the rising popularisation of the paranormal on TV, I was flown up to Aberdeen, Scotland, to discuss this case. Here I discovered the TV researchers had done their job well and added a twist to the tale. Old records had been discovered that had uncovered a lifeboat disaster on this remote bay a century back –- possible further candidates for our bearded sailor ghost. That is if we assume that our bearded sailor was any more substantial than the legendary mermaid claimed to be seen by Sandy Gunn.

Ghost or no ghost is to some extent irrelevant. It was this Sandwood Bay road trip that helped me join important organisations and led me to become (if such a thing exists) a bona fide paranormal researcher. To emphasize the point, I would hope the reader would allow me the license to a very short 'self-quote' from an unpublished poem of mine called 'The Analogy'. A poem about ambitions and dreams which makes this point well — but perhaps without the 'beauty' of the prose of Proust:

> Though many eagerly 'Shovel Coal' at thirteen ... few manage to drive their 'Steam Train'.

I will now end this chapter by noting that perhaps I was now actually driving my 'Steam Train'.

The big question was how far would it travel, and in what direction would the tracks from Sandwood Bay lead?

Chapter 2

Influences!
(Meetings with remarkable people)

I explained in Chapter One that we are subjected to influences, be they from people to our religions or our culture of beliefs. These influences affect the way we comprehend things that can't be explained. So despite leaving Chapter One hanging with the analogy of my paranormal 'train' travelling in a direction as yet undefined, it is essential to first explore this important aspect that other people's influences had. This will give some context to the direction I finally took.

The subtitle to this current chapter, 'Meetings with remarkable people', is a play on words on the book of 'influences' written by the Russian mystic George Ivanovich Gurdjieff, who lived between c 1870 and 1949, and whose book *Meetings with Remarkable Men*, was published posthumously after his death in 1963. It was also the subject of a feature length movie in 1979 featuring the well-known actors Terrance Stamp and Warren Mitchell as well as the Serbian actor Dragan Maksimović as Gurdjieff.

Gurdjieff, from a humble beginning, was to acquire quite a following during his life. This was based on his philosophy that humans live their lives in a sort of waking sleep. This waking sleep according to Gurdjieff was not an inevitable thing. He believed it is possible to awaken the mind to a higher state of consciousness and in that way achieve full human potential. Similar perhaps to the glimpses of wonder that Proust achieved when eating his Madeleine cake, or I, to some extent, achieved when waking up the morning after in Sandwood Cottage after achieving my 'personal dare'. Gurdjieff, however, believed that through following his methods such glimpses of potential become controllable and not just a spontaneous moment.

For the purposes of this chapter, 'men', of course, in the modern world do not and should not be the full source of people's shaping and influences. Though it is an unfortunate fact that at the time of my learning about the paranormal (and subjects that I think relate to it closely), most people who influenced me were indeed men. Today things are (slowly) changing and I look forward to a time when all genders and races will be far more involved in this fascinating subject. As I have also been an avid reader of other people's ideas, such meetings will include people I have met but also some people whose words have had a great influence on me as well.

The 'remarkable men' that Gurdjieff met in his earlier life included his tutor, Dean Borsh, the Armenian priest Pogossian and Prince Lubovedsky, a Russian prince who impressed Gurdjieff with his knowledge of Metaphysics. Whilst I must give Gurdjieff full credit for explaining the importance of this concept for the coming chapter, I must also choose to omit him from my list.

The writer/philosopher Colin Wilson points out in his book *The Occult* (1979) how the publisher Margaret Anderson, a follower of Gurdjieff, wrote the book *The Unknowable Gurdjieff* in which she contends that:

> the chief fault of the Gurdjieff movement … [is that it is] so profound as to be ultimately unknowable.
> (*The Occult*, p. 528)

This, unfortunately, was my experience as well. I remember one Christmas, while back from university, insisting to my slightly bemused but understanding parents that one of my presents should be a book by this mystic with the strange obscure title of *Beelzebub's Tales to His Grandson: An Objectively Impartial*

Criticism of the Life of Man. My sister's boyfriend at the time was a practical man who worked as an electrician. I can remember him flipping through a few pages of this book, rolling his eyes, and saying it all looked just a bit confusing for him. I can also remember, after I struggled through the first two chapters, saying to myself 'Damn it, the man has a point'! Feel free to obtain a copy if you wish to prove me wrong.

Richard Swinburne (born 1934)

One thing Gurdjieff was right about was how a good tutor can have a profound effect on the way that we look at the unexplained parts of life. I mentioned my philosophy professor, Richard Swinburne, in Chapter One and believe that further mention of him is needed. Swinburne is a respected figure and taught at Keele until shortly after my departure. He subsequently became Emeritus Professor of Philosophy at the University of Oxford.

As I previously mentioned, it was under the tuition of Swinburne (whatever his actual views on the subject) that I started to discard a model of science as one that searches for absolute truth. Swinburne oversaw my studies into the philosophy of science and introduced me to the philosopher/scientist Thomas Samuel Kuhn (1922–1996).

Through Kuhn I learnt that throughout the ages we have had what he would term numerous 'Normal Sciences'. These are theories of science that work in a practical sense for a while, are ultimately found to be incorrect or just as importantly incomplete. Ptolemaic theories of how the earth was static at the centre of the Universe were replaced by Copernican Physics, and ultimately by the theories of Newton and then Einstein. This happened, even though all these theories in their time were supported by the leading lights of science and all proved useful in solving problems about the world. Within those 'normal sciences' the proponents of them will defend them vigorously even when their problem-solving ability starts to 'fray'. Kuhn gives an example of this. He points out how aberrations to the Ptolemaic views that the earth was a fixed central point in the universe were explained away by the theory becoming increasingly complex. Proponents of the Ptolemaic view falsely added complex 'epicycles' (circular movements within circular movements) to explain deviations in planetary orbits. This strikes me as about where we are when it comes to excluding the paranormal from science. Objects moving of their own volition (i.e., Poltergeist activity) that are seen by many, are explained by the not yet fully understood concept of mass hallucination or worse by mass fraud. Most scientists rightly dislike 'conspiracy theorists' yet in the better reported poltergeist cases (such as the Enfield poltergeist with at least 30 witnesses) the 'mass fraud' theory starts to sound like a conspiracy theory. Kuhn's psychological and philosophical insights show there is always a new paradigm that will follow the last one and possibly one that could incorporate any 'paranormal' truths.

I was also aware of Swinburne's influence in the philosophy of religion and the attempted later falsification of some of his ideas by Richard Dawkins in that 'politely' named book *The God Delusion* which I mentioned briefly in the Preface. Surprisingly, on one point both philosophers agree.

Swinburne says in his earlier book *Is There a God* (1996), 'It is a hallmark of a simple explanation to postulate few causes. There could in this respect be no simpler explanation than one that postulates one cause' (p. 40).

In doing so Swinburne argues for theism (i.e., One God).

While Dawkins says, 'Science explains complex things in terms of the interactions of simpler things, ultimately the interaction of fundamental particles' (Ch 4, p. 176).

It could be said that Dawkins's God is that of 'fundamental particles' as I am not aware of any justification he gives as to where they came from. His accusations of 'delusions' to those who question the current absolute truth of 'normal science' are certainly said with the fervor of many religious priests or mystical sages.

So, most great thinkers agree that the best theories are based on simple fundamental principles. This is very much not the case when looking at the state of 'paranormal thinking'. Here we have the power of poltergeists, the power of ghosts, and the power of magic, black or white, the power of mediums, the power of sages even to some the power of the Devil. We are left fighting the arguments of both Swinburne and Dawkins. Can we accept lots of chaotic paranormals, or perhaps there is just one overriding theory?

I found it endearing, once, when I watched Swinburne trying to choose an Easter egg (for a friend or a relative?) in the local Keele village shop. Watching him having to ask for advice from the shop assistant as to which Easter egg would suit his needs the best. Our minds can be razor sharp in some areas and a little less so in others. Without such contrast and quirks, I doubt any human could be truly 'remarkable'.

Harry Price (1881–1948)

Now, despite my four or five trips to Transylvania to explore the role of the vampire in the paranormal (of which we will hear more about later), I make no claims to have experienced any strange transformations to everlasting life. Price died in 1948 and my 'meetings' with the man most definitely come through his books and the facts I have learned about him. As he is arguably the founder of modern paranormal research, his influence goes deep, though not without some controversy.

I came across Price while watching the documentary *The Ghost Hunters* which I made mention of in Chapter One. Whilst I was initially interested in Price's Borley Rectory fame, his influence on paranormal research, however, goes much deeper than that.

Influences!

Price could be termed 'the Marmite ghost hunter' either loved or loathed within his field. Even over 70 years after his death, everyone has a different opinion.

Was he the world's most influential ghost hunter to date or an overblown paper bag salesman on a glorified publicity trip? This was the slant used by Richard Morris in his book *Harry Price: The Psychic Detective*. He gave Price that paper bag salesmen's tag and Morris is factually correct in that he was indeed initially employed in a paper bag factory in his younger days.

The problem with this analysis is that virtually all paranormal investigators are basically amateur as we shall see.

To look at what Price did, we must first look at who and what came before. The two best-known so-called ghost hunters before Price came along were Augustus Hare and Elliot O'Donnell. Augustus Hare was the primary source for such famous hauntings as Ham House and the Croglin Grange Vampire. However, when his autobiography was re-published some years back, Walter Kendrick of the *Voice Literary Supplement* pointed out that he was little more than an after-dinner teller of (fabricated?) spooky tales for the rich. Elliot O'Donnell published countless books on ghosts and claimed to be a descendant of Niall of the Nine Hostages, the Irish equivalent of King Arthur. He tended to describe seeing and sometimes fighting with numerous ghosts 'before breakfast'(?), describing them 'objectively' as being featureless blobs of flesh for the reader's delight. So, in the context of Price's predecessors, real paranormal field research possibly didn't exist.

Price first came into the public eye in the 1920s through his investigation of well-known mediums such as Stella Cranshaw and the Schneider Brothers. In the case of the Schneider brothers, Price developed a series of six circuit breakers which would indicate if the medium's arms, legs, hands, or feet had moved.

27

He also developed a pyjama type garment for the medium to wear to preclude the hiding away of things in his clothing.

Now, let's compare all this with a more recent significant investigation into mediums — that of the Scole Report of the Society for Psychical Research. Here the members of the SPR team never searched the mediums, and only easily removable Velcro armbands were used to show that they didn't move around in the dark. So, it seems that even in the early days Price was setting standards which far exceeded those that are often used more recently.

He opened his National Laboratory of Psychical Research in 1926 to his usual media frenzy. It did, however, include as members many respected parapsychologists from around the world.

The laboratory included a library, a photographic studio, and an isolation chamber for testing telekinetic phenomena. It also used 'cutting edge' equipment based on electrical engineering such as electroscopes to detect electrical charges on the body and thermographs to record the continuous changes in temperature. It is only with the coming of cheap computers in the last 20 years that a similar style of equipment has been used again. In between all that, he also had time to revitalise the dormant 'Ghost Club' founded in 1864, which again became a social and discussion hub for serious investigators.

If the way he normally approached investigations can be shown to be sound, much criticism has been made as to his choice of eccentric and publicity generating places which he investigated. One of these was the investigation at Cashen's Gap in the Isle of Man — where the phenomena seemed to be based around a talking mongoose named Gef, who presented himself at the house of the Irving family. Now, although this sounds totally silly at first, many have thought that what the family called Gef may possibly have been a poltergeist that they had given an animal personality to.

Price also observed on a visit that double walls of wooden panelling covered the interior rooms of the house and noted that the unusual build of the house made the whole house one great speaking-tube. This offered a well thought out explanation for either the family spooking themselves or possibly faking phenomena. Put into this context, I fully agree with Price. If a talking mongoose needs investigating, then they should be investigated; if it generates press interest or amusement, then so be it.

Then, of course, there is Borley Rectory itself, which Price investigated for over a decade. The controversy about the haunting of the Rectory and subsequently Borley Church continues to this day. It perhaps encompassed the best and the worst of Price. His flair for (over?) publicity, and use of the press, ensured that coach parties were visiting the rectory for day trips to see the ghost. He did to his credit also conduct a unique experiment of renting out the premises and putting in place a team of observers to capture any phenomena over several months. Whilst some of the instructions to the observers may have been leading, I found that this was my main first reference point when I began my own project of extended witness testimony with regard to the haunting of 'The Cage' at St Osyth, Essex. No person or organisation in the last seven decades had apparently taken on a similar undertaking to that conducted by Price at Borley.

Price has been accused of fraud by some and whilst the evidence for fraud is not conclusive, it is strong enough to say that some of the accusations may be true. His taste for selling books and fame may have later clouded his judgement. Regardless of whether he always followed his own rigorous standards, it is to a large extent those standards that invented modern paranormal research.

So, Price, I think, made a huge and unique contribution — and that wasn't too bad for a man who initially sold paper bags!

Peter Underwood (1923–2014)

Connections between people are interesting things and Peter Underwood wrote in his autobiography, *No Common Task*, how excited he was to meet Harry Price when he was asked to join the Ghost Club, and was in correspondence with Price about a forthcoming meeting. He also wrote of his disappointment when shortly before that meeting he was told that Price had suddenly died. Quite possibly Underwood had received Price's final letter.

Referring to my trip to Sandwood Bay and my correspondence with Underwood (which was normally sent via the London 'Savage Club'), I still have the now somewhat tea-stained reply on official 'Savage Club' notepaper which says: 'Thank you very much indeed for the most interesting report on the Sandwood Bay phenomena which I am delighted to have to add to our files ... I am wondering whether the 'Ghost Club' interests you?'

I joined eagerly and successfully met Peter Underwood at the very next meeting. He was a striking gentleman who could speak for an hour without notes and who for all the time I knew him sported a well-trimmed but slightly goatee beard, which perhaps added to his mystique.

On enquiring about 'Ghost Club' investigations he seemed pleased to encourage my relative mid-20s youth. He informed me that an investigation was taking place within a couple of weeks at a former Airbase called RAF Cosford, which had since that time become an aircraft museum. The base had reported strange experiences on a Lancaster Bomber including the apparent sighting of the figure of an airman in the immediate proximity and in the cockpit. The plane, Lincoln RF 398, had never recorded active service, though Underwood had come across a story which indicated that a pilot had so loved the plane he had stated he would never leave it.

Now, Underwood has often stated that few of his investigations gave him sufficient evidence of the paranormal.

I have also frequently light-heartedly claimed to be about as psychic as the average 'brick'. However, whilst no absolute proof of the paranormal was to occur, there were certainly enough strange happenings to whet my appetite. A detailed account of this investigation can be found in Underwood's book *Nights in Haunted Houses* (1994). Here he points out that 'trigger objects' (objects placed for any paranormal power or entity to move) had frequently been found outside their chalk circles. He also points out that at least two of the team thought they caught sight of the figure of a man. If my memory serves me correctly, one of those team members was him. What he omitted was the thing that jarred my senses most that evening.

Apparently, immediately after these sightings most of the fire exits in the hanger seemed to be open, when previously I'd been certain they had been closed.

Another experience was reported by co-investigator Philip Moore whose report in Peter Underwood's book stated that when he climbed a ladder to the rear of the plane and entered the aircraft, he was immediately confronted 'with a sudden wave of static electricity. It felt as if a wall had been erected and the air was alive' (p. 363).

This description of his experience was to be of particular interest to me in the years to come in forming my impressions of what the 'paranormal' could be.

Perhaps I assumed at that time that this would be one of many interesting investigations I would have with Underwood, who went on to write over 40 books on the subject. However, despite his talents in popularising the paranormal, mostly in a rational and sensible way, he, like Price, was not a man without some flaws. A few years after the RAF Cosford investigation, and when Underwood had been the President of the club for several decades, he had a disagreement with the Chair, Tom Perrot, and Council member Bill Bellars. This provoked his resignation and his setting up a new organisation called the

Ghost Club Society. This split the club in two, with Underwood taking many leading members. The Ghost Club split, in fact, hit parts of the British national press.

Underwood was to invite me to join the Ghost Club Society in a polite telephone call. Perhaps, though, my more than passing interest in politics made me object to the fact that it was his stated intention to be President for life. I politely declined the offer.

Over time, relations thawed, and he was to give me some useful quotes for my first book on paranormal investigation, *Ghost Hunting: A Survivor's Guide* (2010), and though we only met once after the millennium, we remained on friendly terms. I was confident he would assist in writing an article about his life for the popular journal *Fortean Times*. My confidence extended to the point that I had already asked for the help of Ghost Club member Sarah Darnell, who lived, like Underwood, in the small town of Haslemere, Surrey, UK.

I was disappointed but understood when he declined the invitation and stated that 'I am 91 and a half and some days I feel very under the weather and not fit for anything'.

I was far more saddened and shocked when within a week his death was announced on the internet and shortly after in the national press.

As with Price's correspondence to Underwood — perhaps I had also received Underwood's final letter?

Colin Wilson (1932–2013)

Whilst Colin Wilson's flaw was perhaps to state his 'remarkableness' to the world a little too often, his writings on philosophy and the Occult were compiled with such precision but with a storytelling narrative. They could become quite literally an inspiration to read. I 'discovered' him while still in my latter stages of Secondary (High) school. I mainly read his thick green book *The Occult* in the 'alternative' chill out area that was officially the computer room, which few schools had at the turn of the 1980s. Few of us that hung out in the room actually used that cutting edge computer, even when it evolved from using ticker tape to tele-printer then finally to an actual TV monitor. Wilson's book proved much more of a catalyst for people's attention, especially from a fascinating female art student, who when spotted my reading material introduced me to weekly meetings of a strange cult called the Emin.

The Emin was a society founded by a man called Raymond Armin who preferred to go by the Emin name of 'Leo', and whose teachings were based on finding the 'Eminent Way' (shortened to 'Emin'). These were continued through the 1970s with the help of his son John Armin ('Orman') who prior to that had been a boot polish salesman. This background seemed strangely similar in some ways to that of Harry Price.

The Emin believed in spiritual development through a hierarchical system of 16 spheres, each representing a level of consciousness. This was in many ways like the writings of Wilson who very much believed that we live our life in a 'waking sleep' and can occasionally reach 'Peak Experience' through what he called Faculty X.

Whilst there may have been a similarity of message, what I felt was an unquestioning indoctrinating approach was highly unsuitable for my (over?) enquiring mind. I was given the Emin name of 'Spiral' (I suspect they envisaged it would be a long and winding road for me) but doubt that in the weeks I attended I even got to the second sphere. After some weeks, I told my art student friend what I perceived of as dangers and extracted myself from the Emin — though she continued for a while. One Sunday paper was to, shortly after, run an 'exposé' about the Emin when a worried parent contacted them after my art student friend introduced someone else from school.

Wilson's books were far more than just a 'magnet' in making interesting acquaintances. As an example of this, it was he who managed to explain to me what Gurdjieff was all about, in a way I felt that Gurdjieff himself could not. He most importantly made connexions between changes of states of mind and strange phenomena occurring. This is a point which is covered more fully in my book *Poltergeists: A New Investigation into Destructive Haunting* (2019). Which to sum up my respect for Wilson is a play on the title of one of his books, *Poltergeist: A study of Destructive Haunting* (1981).

He was a long-standing member of the Ghost Club but when the club split, he joined Peter Underwood's new organisation — so I sadly was only able to meet him once when he gave a talk.

I asked him if it was possible to join a group to follow his philosophical ideas and he politely told me there were no such groups and that seeking esoteric truths was a lone endeavour. He was incorrect on this one point at least. There have been Colin Wilson groups and conferences that have still been set up since his death.

Maurice Grosse, and Guy Playfair
(1919–2006) / (1935–2018)

Maurice and Guy are two very different people but will continue to be uttered in the same sentence by many, simply because of the unique investigation they were to conduct at the Enfield Poltergeist House in the 1970s. At the time Maurice was a recently retired inventor, whose motivation to investigate was partly due to the recent bereavement of his daughter. Guy was an author who had just returned from extensive paranormal research in Brazil. It was these natural gaps in their lives, along with the cooperation of the Hodgson family and a very active case, that was to allow many months of research when most of us can manage only a few days or weeks. The witness pool extended beyond the immediate family to journalists, policemen, and neighbours, as well as Grosse and Playfair.

It even included a visit from Demonologists Ed and Lorraine Warren, whose portrayal of Enfield in the movie *The Conjuring 2* not surprisingly went from poltergeist case to that of a malevolent demon.

The depth and width of evidence of Enfield put the incidents into what I would call a Fact or Fraud scenario. Too many objects moving for illusion so either paranormal (fact) or a very clever fraud indeed, and that I think is the essence of any very interesting case. Grosse and Playfair were convinced but others saw the two young teenage girls in the house playing tricks. As the more sceptical psychologist Chris French stated in an interview in *Time Out* magazine: 'The spirit of an old man, Bill, who possessed Janet, was obsessed with periods' (www.timeout.com/london/blog).

I was to meet both Grosse and Playfair on frequent occasions a couple of decades after the case, as co-members of the Society for Psychical Research (SPR) Council and also of the SPR Spontaneous Cases Group.

I personally found Grosse, whilst inclined to believe in phenomena, both charming and open minded. I discovered that he had been excluded from the previous long running Scole experiment in physical mediumship, for posing non afterlife theories which were against the mediums' systems of beliefs. I suspect he too would have lasted only a short number of weeks in the 'Emin'.

Playfair was also charming but a little more reserved. His work on poltergeists both before and after Enfield were to prove to be an inspiring base for further research in the future. This applies especially to his work in Brazil where he categorized poltergeist incidents and initially noticed a difference in style between poltergeist knocks and raps and those by other means. These acoustic differences have been further explored by SPR Council Member Barry Colvin amongst others.

Mary Rose Barrington 1926–2020

Barrington was a stalwart of the SPR council which she joined in 1962 (before I was born) and which she stayed on till near the end of her life. She was a wonderful lady of 'fierce independent' mind at a time when it would have been far less fashionable to be so. As well as an accomplished paranormal researcher, Barrington also worked as a barrister and perhaps struck me as one of the most intelligent people I had met since my tutor Richard Swinburne.

Barrington's main inspiration to me was her works on JOTTs. Low level (possibly) supernatural events that are put down as (J)ust (O)ne of (T)hose (T)hings such as objects disappearing and reappearing in impossible places. This opens, at least, the possibility that the paranormal may indeed be common and all around us.

I remember that the SPR Conference held in 2015 at Greenwich University had very strong winds coming from the River Thames outside the lecture hall and seeing a now frail Mary Rose struggling against a gust. I remember thinking of going to help her but then deciding that a person of fierce independence might not appreciate such assistance. Mary Rose, of course, arrived for the lecture calm and collected and in good time.

Nicolae Paduraru (1937–2009)

I would be parodying what Nicolae was to simply call him a former senior member of the Ministry for Tourism in Romania during communist times. Though he was indeed this and took his responsibilities for looking after foreign guests seriously. These included the well-known actor Peter Gilmore, who starred in the UK hit television series *The Onedin Line* in the early 1970s.

Nicolae also became fascinated by the growing numbers of western travellers that wanted to seek out non-existent buildings in and around Transylvania. Written about in the 'banned' book *Dracula* by Bram Stoker. His rational 'Communist' mind perhaps challenged by the dreams and imaginations of others. Yet like something akin to the *Field of Dreams* film starring Kevin Costner, (where a farmer builds a baseball field in his cornfield and people come in their droves to see it), Nicolae with the help of his colleagues even persuaded the Communist leader Ceausescu to build a Castle Dracula Hotel on the remote hills of the Borgo Pass. This was after all where Bram Stoker stated Dracula's Castle should be — and, strangely, people from all over the world came to visit in awe.

In the late 1990s after communism fell, the Ghost Club was looking for something 'different' to explore and we tracked down Nicolae's new organisation, the Transylvanian Society of Dracula, with whom we toured the delightful sights of legend. I was later to cooperate with him in organising other group tours which included liaising with the Hammer House of Horror actress Ingrid Pitt and persuading her to attend the World Dracula Congress near the wonderful medieval town of Brasov. I had thought at first that Nicolae's romantic side had given me too much of a challenge here. However, perhaps my charming emails and telephone calls combined by Nicolae's ex-communist connections to get Ms Pitt first-class passage on Romanian Airways ensured she did attend.

Now whilst this is partially a book about my romantic dreams of the paranormal, my experiences with Nicolae went beyond that simple aspect. Nicolae who was officially an atheist from his communist background had an inquisitive open mind. He called stray dogs 'sir' out of respect — I believe just in case they were a reincarnation of someone deserving from a previous life. He also kept good contacts with Romanian universities who were experimenting with things such as Kirlean Photography which some believe can show the power and health of the human 'Aura'.

One of the most remarkable parts of my many trips to Romania was learning to see the variety of ways different cultures talk about the same phenomena. What we might call a poltergeist case they, until at least recently, might call a vampire attack — but take away the linguistics and we still have the same phenomenon. This, I believe, is key to understanding the paranormal.

Whether my trips to Romania and in particular my night in the Castle Dracula Hotel kept me 'youthful in mind and body', I will, of course, leave for others to decide.

Robert M. Pirsig (1928–2017)

I have never met Mr Pirsig and sadly never will and at first glance we may seem strange bedfellows as Richard Dawkins uses a quote from Pirsig's second book, *Lila: An Inquiry into Morals*, in his previously mentioned book *The God Delusion*: 'When one person suffers from a delusion it is called insanity, when many people suffer from a delusion it is called religion' (p 28).

However, it is Pirsig's first inspiring book, *Zen and the Art of Motorcycle Maintenance*, that perhaps helped clarify my thought process on how the mind works. A book that *Street Life* reviewed and recommended should be read: 'On the road … a mountainside, the bottom of an ocean … read the goddamn thing [it's] the very heart of things.'

It is a compliment to this book that I still remember exactly where I finished it. Not at the bottom of the ocean, but on a very slow long train journey from Stuttgart to Dusseldorf. This was completed when travelling between matches in the 1988 soccer European Championships in Germany. Here I was also to finally 'represent' England in goal during a 'friendly' fans' match against Ireland.

The book is not about Buddhism and not a motorcycle manual but involves a 'meditation' around a real road trip (to self-discovery) by motorcycle, combined with numerous philosophical discussions including on the philosophy of science. The real twist is the third narrative, that of Pirsig's own mental breakdown, caused by his left brain just thinking too damned much. This happened to me, to a less significant extent in my mid-teens. I would spend what seemed like hours on the bus home thinking why should I do this, why should I do that, until I finally came up with the answer. If no harm is done to others, I should do what pleases me, and hell it doesn't please me to sit here sitting in a stupor, so, left brain, please F*** off! This is a fine philosophical statement that I can use to this day every time I become a little OCD.

I believe that finding the truth about anything and especially those things thought of as 'paranormal' needs both intellect and 'inspiration' from a well-balanced mind.

My thinking is that Pirsig recognised this fact, as he was accompanied on this road trip by his friend John Sutherland. Sutherland is portrayed as less interested in obsessing about the minutiae of how his own motorcycle works and of experiencing the moment. In effect, the 'romantic' right side of the brain personified.

Sutherland and Pirsig combined would make the perfect paranormal investigator. Reading about their adventures and Pirsig's underlying thoughts was nothing short of inspirational. Even Dawkins in *The God Delusion* talks about looking up at the stars and being 'dazzled by Orion ... and Ursa Major ... Tearful with the unheard music of the Milky Way' (pp. 31–32).

Yet, it seems some such as Dawkins at least can't jump from that peak experience to the small possibility that there might be 'something else'!

Before this chapter closes, I will also make mention of **Hugh Pincott** who helped me greatly in my first tentative steps in exploring the mind through hypnotic regression. The only reason this mention is brief is so as not to ruin the very next chapter. I should also make mention of **Rosie O'Carroll** for her skilful assistance in many investigations, along with her brother **Alan Murdie** who after the split in the Ghost Club took it from strength to strength as (elected) Chair.

When it comes to remarkable people in my life, a certain **Dominique Fraser** is more than deserving of this all too brief mention as well.

Every successful journey, after all, depends on your fellow travellers!

Chapter 3

An Idea Born or Reborn?
(Discovering strange powers through hypnotic regression)

In the latter part of my teenage years, I started to subscribe to a slim weekly newspaper called *Psychic News*. It was basically a newspaper for those whose views were that of spiritualists and believers in the afterlife, as opposed to a journal of scientific enquiry. Once that fact was accepted it made for an interesting read and there were few other magazines at the time that ventured into such areas.

An incident in 1984 involving the *Psychic News* is also a good example of the need to tread carefully between that tempting path of outright belief and that of the hard-line sceptic. This involved the emerging psychic who went under the name of Zwinge and who visited the *Psychic News* offices at that time. He proceeded to make clocks go forward as well as bending spoons and knives. *Psychic News* reported these incidents with great positivity, as if a new Uri Geller-type psychic had been discovered. Clearly he looked the part. According to the book *The Magic of Uri Geller* (1975), *Psychic News* described him as a man 'with ... grey beard, intense eyes ... [and] magnetic aura' (p. 259).

The grey bearded individual was soon to reveal himself as the famous debunking magician James Randi — perhaps the actual nemesis of Geller, and the author of the above-named book.

Whilst everything one read in the *Psychic News* should not have always been accepted at face value, its purchase price was more than covered in a 1981 edition. It was an editorial piece about a new organisation that had just been set up called ASSAP

(Association for the Scientific Study of Anomalous Phenomena) and came complete with an application form.

The long and cumbersome name of ASSAP came from the wish to have an interdisciplinary approach to things currently 'anomalous' to science, and to end the separation of research into such things as UFOs, ghosts and poltergeists. In effect, to look at the paranormal as one joined up discipline. The founders knew of no short title that would encapsulate such a novel concept, so ASSAP became the name. This is also a concept that I gradually realised could be key to our understanding of (potentially) one big paranormal box of tricks — one paranormal power expressing itself in various ways.

Unlike other organisations at the time ASSAP ran training days. Perhaps with the 'James Randi' episode in the *Psychic News* still in the back of my mind, I decided to go on one about fraud and faked phenomena. Whilst at the event, I confidently pointed out that a fake 'table tipping' session was caused by a simple conjurer's misdirection — only to be shown that it was caused by small retractable poles on a bracelet device that slid under the table which ensured it was naturally tilted on command. I also had the pleasure of a first meeting with Maurice Grosse of Enfield fame, who helped set up and participate in this trick. He was not a man to exclude himself to one organisation only, which sadly was common at the time. The unfortunate fact was that one of several reasons for the founding of ASSAP was a perceived disillusionment of some as to the old-fashioned nature of the SPR. I was not a member of the SPR then, so make no judgement on that.

ASSAPs founding members included prominent SPR researcher Vernon Harrison, former President of the Royal Photographic Society. They also included no less than the former Honorary Secretary and Treasurer of the SPR, the accomplished scientist (Chartered Chemist) Hugh Pincott who at the time was assistant coordinator of BPs chemicals operation in the Western Hemisphere.

I ran into Hugh at several meetings and found him to be a charming man who was keen to involve younger members in ongoing research. Once I had finished my degree at Keele, and returned to London, I was more than happy to help participate in weekly experiments he was conducting into hypnotic regression and the possible past life hypothesis.

These weekly meetings consisted of six or seven people and were conducted at Hugh's large flat in Blackheath, a more fashionable suburb of Southeast London. The format was democratic and open with the participants swapping their roles week to week. These consisted of being the note taker (known as 'scribe'), recording the sessions or being a hypnotic subject, and to ultimately being trained in hypnotic techniques under the watchful eye of very experienced hypnotists. Normally by 10 p.m. we would retire to the pub to socialise and talk about our progress.

From the group's past experiences, it was thought possible to get the average subject into deep trance within six or seven sessions, or even quicker with a technique known as the 'Velvet Hammer'. As the weeks progressed though, it seemed clear to me that I was not the 'average subject'. Even with a 'Velvet Hammer' probing my mind, my inquisitive left brain would not turn off. I was in some kind of trance but still very aware of my surroundings. This was not a success for regression but was a fascinating experience that gave me a great deal of insight into the process.

When I was in my state of light to medium trance, it became very clear in my conscious mind that I had a great desire to 'please' the hypnotist. I had a desire to become what he or she wanted and to conjure up images and ideas that assisted that aim. This light trance state of mind gave me a great deal

of insight into both the power of hypnosis and possibly its
weakness in bringing out real-life facts.

This is a debate that continues in hypnotherapy to this day,
particularly about forgotten memories of serious incidents such
as sexual abuse. Some practitioners believe that the memory
works like a video camera, and it is simply a question of accessing
those accurate 'video archives' deep in the mind. However, to
quote the eminent psychologist Dr Elizabeth Hartney:

> The mind is not like a video camera; it is more like a
> scrapbook, whereby memories are created by combining
> pieces of sensory experience with interpretation and fantasy.
> (verywellmind.com/can-hypnosis-unlock-memories-of-
> childhood-abuse)

This was very much my own personal interpretation of the
hypnotic process which of course has implications when dealing
with past life regression theories. This interpretation was only
strengthened when I gradually got trained, under supervision,
in hypnotic techniques. I got interesting stories from the average
subjects I dealt with, but nothing so specific as to be worth
mentioning in this book. In fact, the 'success' I remember best
was with the subject's prior permission persuading him that
the cigarettes that he chain-smoked would taste like burning
rubber for the next week. He was very grateful when in fact
they did!

Of equal interest to this theory was a session in which I was
the scribe. In this case there was no reference to regression,
simply to take the female subject (whom we will refer to as
'Lucy') through a tunnel and to see where she appeared. Here
the subject emerged according to my notes, fully submerged
underwater as a mermaid. She found herself in front of a sunken
ship called the Winged Dolphin on which she discovered
sunken treasure including a magical golden spear. The magical

spear that 'Lucy' was sure she could use to become fully human again. This shows how powerful the fantasy angle can be when memories are not requested. A wonderful story of romance designed to please an audience of 'romantic' paranormal investigators. Who can seriously say that even under hypnotic guidance to a past life scenario that this desire to please with fantasy suddenly disappears?

Whilst the sessions I attended provided very limited 'past life regression' success, there was often discussion about a previous subject who for personal reasons had to withdraw from the group. This was a subject whose recollections should really be at the forefront of the hypnotic regression debate. A retired senior school inspector who will go under the pseudonym of Don Brown, whose speciality in the classroom was geography. This was a subject who could get into the deep trance state that I could not attain. A subject who could literally take on new personas; in particular one that claimed to be Cerdic the Saxon.

Like all initial subjects, Don Brown was initially taken slowly back through his current life where at the age of eleven he amused the group with his colourful accounts of selling programmes at a cricket match in Canterbury. When taken prior to his birth date, Don Brown took on initially the persona of a Harold Dickenson from Wrexham, who in 1913 became a medical student at the University of Cardiff. Harold proved to be of interest as he gave out a lot of checkable facts such as regiment details and officers' names. Harold was later to die in battle during the First World War.

Unfortunately, many of the facts during later research on 'Harold Dickenson' proved to be incorrect. The officers' names did not exist which very much supports the theory of hypnotism that I mentioned earlier. However, other details were far more impressive. These included Harold's daily walk to University College, past Cardiff Castle and other accurate landmarks in a town that Don Brown had never travelled to. This is of particular interest as Hugh Pincott was very familiar with the town and possibly at least an indication that Don Brown was getting information from somewhere else, not yet explained by science — possibly telepathically from Hugh himself. Perhaps there was more to hypnotic regression than simply taking someone to a past life?

I have discussed in previous chapters the concept of triggers altering our state of consciousness, and few would argue about hypnosis being one of the strongest triggers of all. Could it possibly be in such altered states that strange inexplicable things also start to happen, things that most would deem to be paranormal?

During future sessions the group gradually regressed Don Brown further back in time. They noted that he still had enough 'self-identity' to be genuinely startled when he took on the persona of someone of the opposite sex — a lady called Arabella who lived in the 1700s. As Don Brown went yet further back in time, finally the persona of Cerdic the Saxon appeared.

At first the group had no special expectations about this persona, though in deep trance as always Don Brown was most forthcoming with the smallest of details. Cerdic was of minor Anglo Saxon nobility, what was known at the time as a thegn and resided in Wrotham in Kent, a place that certainly exists. The group first 'met' Cerdic in 1033 as a young man of nineteen. He was happy to go into detail about the harsh times he lived through. Of interest to note was the fact that Cerdic was also happy to use the modern calendar, and like the possibly Polish ghost at Sandwood Bay was able to speak in very understandable English rather than communicate in pure Anglo-Saxon dialect.

The group were in some ways a little disappointed when Cerdic's life progressed towards its climax at the Battle of Hastings in 1066. It is perhaps the cliché of past life regression that few of the personas that communicate have dull and ordinary lives. I wonder how many have had past lives as Napoleon or Cleopatra, and would say that, relatively speaking, our Blackheath group had escaped the cliché lightly.

However, this posed a unique opportunity to actually get hold of a history book and check the facts on the spot. 'Cerdic' got the obscure but recorded details correct. These included fighting for King Harold under the banner of a dragon. To quote Hugh Pincott's detailed report: 'It was almost as though Don Brown was reading the [history] book telepathically through my eyes.'

He also stated that the night before the battle was 'a bright clear sky ... stars, a quarter moon'.

Cerdic correctly pointed out that Halley's Comet (as seen in the famous Bayeux tapestry on the eve of battle) was not there but that such a great fire in the sky had happened seven or eight months prior.

Even though Don Brown had no background in history, Cerdic the Saxon could well have been renamed Cerdic the Historian. Nearly all the facts that could be checked were basically right. Of equal interest was the observation that over many hypnotic sessions the facts of Cerdic's life stayed totally consistent.

Cedric was therefore 'of interest' with regard to a past life hypothesis, but perhaps far more so using an alternative hypothesis that hypnosis (as well as other things) can alter the state of the mind and unlock hidden talents, possibly of a paranormal type. We have seen strong hints in the descriptions above of what could be hypnotically-induced ESP — the ability to pick up the thoughts of others, especially in this case, the hypnotist. This, though, was not the only talent that Don Brown started to show.

With the emergence of the persona of Cedric there was also the emergence of a hidden artist as well. Prior to the 'Cerdic' sessions, Don Brown had just been a doodler of no great talent at all. To quote from Hugh's report again, 'he did so with a precise geometric dot and angle pattern characterising a precise and logical mind'. This is typical 'left brain' behaviour.

Once Cerdic appeared, his style of drawing totally changed and he became a high-speed artist of some distinction, graphically portraying the life of Cerdic the Saxon. Don Brown also started portraying the life of Cedric in automatic writing in a strange archaic style. As if the power of hypnosis had awakened the more creative right side of his mind.

Automatic art has a history of developing in parallel with other aspects of the paranormal. Perhaps one of the best-known cases is that of Mathew Manning, which is covered in greater depth in my previous book on poltergeists. Manning as a young boy was plagued by poltergeist incidents both at home and at his boarding school, which nearly led to his expulsion for the disruption it caused. In later adolescence, he appeared to communicate with 'spirits' including that of a Henrietta Webb who claimed to have resided in the family's historical house in Linton, Cambridgeshire, UK, during the seventeenth century. At the same time as this, Manning started experiencing bouts of automatic drawing and writing. The writing coming in languages such as Greek and Arabic which he had little or no knowledge of.

I hope the reader can forgive me for using a quote from my previous book where Manning explains the process he used prior to tuning in to his newfound talents:

> I empty my mind as completely as possible and, in that state, I think of the person I am trying to contact — sending all that energy out to the person who then writes and draws with my hand.
> (*The Link*, Mathew Manning, 1975, p. 125)

The reason this quote fascinates me so much is that it seems close to a process of changing one's state of consciousness. Close even to a form of self-hypnosis.

There are many other examples of this creative force. One of these is that of the psychic Rosemary Brown. Brown communicated with what she believed were the spirits of famous composers including Chopin and Liszt amongst many others. These composers in particular seemed to guide her hands automatically to create new musical works. Whilst these seemed perfectly in the style of the musicians, they also seemed, according to most music experts, to add little to their existing compilations. Even if Brown's creations were from her subconscious mind it remains a good example of the mind's hidden powers.

Don Brown and Manning and for that matter Rosemary Brown had their skills developed in different ways. With Don Brown attaining his through that of a 'past life' experience, Manning through initial poltergeist type phenomena and Rosemary Brown through a belief in more conventional spiritualist mediumship. Could it nevertheless be that the skills that were awakened were really one and the same?

Taken from the same box of (sometimes) paranormal powers but expressed in different ways?

Hugh Pincott wrote a detailed and what he called 'interim' report on the phenomena and a video based on the recordings of Cerdic. However, after Don Brown left the hypnotic regression group no subsequent subjects — certainly not me — were to be as remotely interesting. Hugh ultimately moved away from London running a niche book ordering service on the paranormal called Specialist Knowledge Services and used his in-depth knowledge in a way that could be so useful in those pre-Amazon times. He does, however, remain a member of ASSAP and is still active in research through the Afterlife Research

Trust whose current projects include an attempt to 'artificially' create a poltergeist by the name of Quentin Peacock. This is an attempt to replicate the famous 'Philip' experiment of which more will be said later. For now, however, please do not try this at home.

Without the expertise of Hugh Pincott, this important and underreported experiment in hypnotic regression came to a halt. With the interim report apparently becoming the group's final word on the subject — at least for a long period of time.

Recently, I re-read the report and became fascinated by the drawings. Many of which appear in the hard to obtain video which sadly has been partially corrupted. The moving images are blurred but the still-life drawings and the commentary, thankfully, are clear.

I was looking for any that might convey places or facts that could be in any way checkable. The first thing I found was an interesting statement from Cerdic. It was concerning a particularly excruciating form of execution known as the 'Blood Eagle'. This consisted of separating the victim's ribs from their spine and bones and positioning them outward to form a set of eagle-like wings. Cerdic was clear that this practice had been stopped by the holy King Edward the Confessor who reigned from 1042–1066. He stated that it had previously been allowed by his evil predecessor, Harthacnut (1040–1042), second son of the more famous King Cnut the Great who in legend tried to keep back the sea. This was a particularly interesting 'fact check' for those such as me who have quite recently watched the *Vikings': The Saga of Ragnar Lothbrok* which recently appeared on Prime TV. These sagas presented the 'Blood Eagle' as an important form of ritualised punishment, when prior to that, I believe that few would have even heard of such a thing.

Such apparently solid facts provided by Cerdic were not so solid when it came to checking them out in known history. The concept of the 'Blood Eagle' comes from only about nine sources in the literature of the real Viking sagas. On the plus side, at least Harthacnut was part of a Viking Dynasty known as the House of Denmark, who had taken the English Crown after invading in 1013. The few historical accounts in relation to the 'Blood Eagle' were mainly written a long time after the event and it is unclear whether the punishment was real in the literal way suggested.

Historian Ronald Hutton, in his book *The Pagan Religions of the Ancient British Isles*, believes it to be a Christian myth based on a misreading of an old text. It could also be propaganda against the 'old ways' that Cerdic spoke a lot about as well. Even if the 'Blood Eagle' existed there is only one recorded incident I could track down of it happening on English soil. This was when the sons of Ragnar Lothbrok executed King Ælla of Northumbria in AD 867 in revenge for the killing of their father. There is no evidence that such practices continued into the eleventh century.

What we therefore seem to have when it comes to Don Brown taking on Cerdic's persona is inexplicably good access to unexpected outside information, with regard to an obscure historical form of punishment and many other details. When no details can be found, Cerdic appears to indulge in creative storytelling to fill in the missing bits. In effect, like the subject 'Lucy' he creates his own 'magical spear'. Edward the Confessor was a good Anglo Saxon like Cerdic, who replaced the 'evil' (in Cerdic's eyes) Danish Viking dynasty. What better way to portray an 'evil' dynasty than to represent it as sanctioning those evil barbaric 'Blood Eagle' executions?

There was also one further picture in which I thought there might be checkable facts. These consisted of a view of Rochester Town and Bridge. They portrayed Rochester Bridge as a distinct bridge with turrets and a distinct settlement of no great size but with a round protective low fenced ditch, perhaps being added at some point to protect its strategic importance? Could there be any records of the bridge and settlement? This was, after all, just after the end of the largely unrecorded 'Dark Ages'.

Rochester is a fascinating town in Kent which I happen to know rather well. It is dominated by the ruins of its Norman castle built after that famous Battle of Hastings by William the conquering king. It also has Watling Street, a key Roman road going under the High Street and visible via the basement of what is now a tattoo parlour. It is known that Watling Street led to the Roman bridge which was a key point to cross the river Medway. The history of the town after the castle was built in 1087 is also well established, but prior to that there is something of a historical gap.

The obvious first point of contact was the local Guildhall Museum who pointed out that by a stroke of luck there was an organisation known as the Rochester Bridge Trust. This was set up in the fourteenth century to fund the maintenance of a new bridge after an older one had been washed away in floods. Further enquiries with the trust were to become far more revealing, in that the bridge that washed away was in fact the Roman one that had been so well built it had survived for over a millennium. It would therefore have been the very same bridge that Cerdic himself had crossed. The foundations of the Roman bridge have also been found and from that and historical records it is believed to be a bridge with protective turrets at either side, tantalisingly like the graphic portrayal by Cerdic.

Again, by good luck the trust had held an art competition in 2019 to depict the bridge, with the artists being fed information from the Trust's appointed experts. The winning entry can be found at: https://rbt.org.uk/2019/interpretations-of-the-roman-bridge-at-rochester/.

Not only does this depict the bridge much like Cerdic portrayed in his artwork but also shows a settlement south of the river of an insubstantial size, but with substantial circular *brick* defences as well. There is also a strong tradition in post Roman Europe of superior Roman brickwork being dismantled and used for other projects, the best example being the slow destruction of the 73-mile defensive wall built by the emperor Hadrian. So, take away the protective wall of Rochester Village over the next 1000 years and you are left with Cerdic's pictorial description exactly.

It seems with regard to Cerdic that when the knowledge is potentially available, even when the knowledge is very obscure, that determined Saxon persona would inevitably find it. When it comes to what that 'persona' is, Hugh Pincott favoured to a large extent what he termed the 'Fly Paper' theory. This is a theory that there are latent personalities within us that contain our hidden hopes and dreams that get externalised through the 'Fly paper' or catalyst of powerful hypnotic trance. Hugh, in his paper, gives ad hoc examples of this such as a bus conductor who might have had ambitions to be a deep-sea explorer and whose hypnotised past life persona would in some way reflect that fact. I could add to that 'hypothetical' list an ex-internal auditor soon to be credit manager with not so latent desires to be a goalkeeper, paranormal investigator and even occasionally a Member of Parliament as well. I can't help wondering what personas would have emerged if such a subject had ever got to deep trance?

From my experiences mentioned so far, I was also starting to discover that when the mind is reset in such a way hidden powers start to emerge. These can be impressive natural powers and possibly paranormal ones as well. With regard to the possible paranormal ones, is there not a point when it starts to sound even more absurd, when it comes to Cerdic, that Don Brown had prior knowledge of such obviously obscure facts? Would it not be more 'scientific' to at least accept the possibility that he somehow picked them up using powers not yet fully understood?

Arthur Conan Doyle perhaps puts it better in *The Case Book of Sherlock Holmes*: 'When you have eliminated all which is impossible, then whatever remains, however improbable, must be the truth.'

When that point comes, you have a new paradigm of science that at least needs to try to include that which was previously shunned by the 'old' science!

After the Ghost Club split in two, for several years I was not active in the new organisation. I can remember being re-inspired in the latter part of the 1990s when I woke up with a headache one Sunday morning, having been out the previous night. I decided, reluctantly at first, to drag myself along to a brunch time gathering in honour of our long-standing Chair Tom Perrot. The gathering turned out to be an all-day champagne and canapés party, held in the garden of an exclusive mansion house in fashionable Chelsea and generously hosted by one of the Ghost Clubs newer members. I am a little vague at which point in the afternoon I was suddenly re-inspired. At some point I accepted an offer in principle for the post of Vice-Chair (Investigations) which I took up on Tom's forthcoming retirement. Tom was replaced by ghost hunting barrister Alan Murdie, who still holds this post today.

After working with Guy Playfair, Maurice Grosse, and Mary Rose Barrington on the Spontaneous Cases Committee of the SPR, I was subsequently, in 2008, also offered a place on the SPR Ruling Council. Certainly, an honour of at least equal status to that of my Ghost Club one, but one that came without the persuasion of a surreal all-day champagne garden party.

At the time I became Vice-Chair of the Ghost Club in 1999 we had no events officer, so I also took on the role of assisting and finding speakers from the club. One of the speakers was a sceptical but open-minded psychologist by the name of Chris French, who I have frequently run into since on other occasions. He had returned from filming a documentary on beliefs and evidence for reincarnation amongst the Druze people of Lebanon, a small religious group which accepts the concept fully.

Chris French, being a sceptic, came out with potentially rational explanations for the cases that he had interviewed. Problematic issues do indeed exist with the Druze interpretation of past lives. These include the facts that

1. Transition from one life to another must be in an instant, which may lead a community of believers to literally seeking out a past life based on this exact timing.
2. That transition must be from one Druze to another Druze. For a small community of less than one million worldwide, who stopped accepting converts in 1043 AD, there is a significant chance that the past life came from a place that is known or nearby.
3. Most of the best memories come from young children closest to their previous lives but also not the most reliable of witnesses.

Unlike some more dogmatic sceptics, French tended to argue, at that time, that regardless of the truth of such religious theories, believing in reincarnation is beneficial for the Druze on a psychological and social level. If it bonds a society together, a culture of reincarnation surely does no harm. This is something those fellow sceptics such as Dawkins should take note of.

My interest in the subject produced further research and an interesting fact from Erlendur Haraldsson, the well-known Icelandic parapsychologist. Haraldsson has done a comprehensive survey on the character traits of such children. He makes particular note of the fact that past life children: 'Tend to be preoccupied with their thoughts or with daydreaming' (*The Journal of Nervous and Mental Disease*, Vol 200, No 11, Nov 2012).

This has a familiar ring, as being, at least, to some extent a light touch opening of the subconscious mind, possibly even a state of light self-hypnosis. Not quite enough to compose music in the style of long dead composers as achieved by Rosemary Brown. Perhaps through a small percentage of daydreaming children open their subconscious minds just enough to recollect some overheard fact about someone who had died just before they were born?

A final interesting fact on this subject is a claim with which, when I trained in hypnosis, I became familiar. This is the fairly well-established claim that only about 5–10% of people are highly susceptible to hypnosis. It does after all make for a good explanation of the reason why some stage magicians try an initial hypnotic trick on the whole audience and only call those special 5–10% group onto the stage that show good results in the initial phase. This was equally shown in my hypnotic regression group where there were clearly some star performers. It also leads to an even more interesting question.

What if roughly this percentage of people is also equally susceptible to unexplained talents and experiences being triggered in them in other ways?

What if the act of hypnotism and hypnotic regression is simply one key to that magic box of tricks?

Chapter 4

The Strange 'Art' of Ghost Hunting
(Not quite a science despite generations of trying?)

In 1992 I found myself in between jobs and reasonably financially secure. With the timing right, I decided to aim for one of the things that had been on my 'bucket list' of things to do in life. I gained selection for the Croydon North-East Constituency as a parliamentary candidate for the Liberal Democrat party. I had never expected to win but did come a respectable third place, and overall got reasonable press coverage. The local press were bored of people in suits and as one of the candidates still under 30 years old, wanted to photograph me in pursuit of one of my hobbies. Ghost hunting came with too many diverting questions, so, as I still played football to a competitive recreational level, I ended up being photographed holding a football wearing the full goalkeeping regalia. The headline I believe was 'A Safe Pair of Hands for Croydon' — though whether it ended with a question mark (?) or an explanation mark (!) I really cannot remember.

My activities in politics at that time are only occasionally hinted at in this book to show my life had a strange but sometimes interesting balance. I mention this briefly now, in the context of this chapter, as politics is fully accepted as a subjective 'art'. Full of facts, full of strong beliefs but definitely opinion led with any hunt for truth being replaced with a hunt for the popular vote.

The question I was starting to wonder was, when it came to day-to-day ghost hunting, were the results simply like politics, a subjective 'art' as well?

Ghost hunting, like politics, has its celebrities and stars. Though for many ghost hunters the celebrities and stars are (sadly) not the people who write books on the subject. To a slightly lesser extent, (at least in the UK), neither are they the people who front the numerous television shows that have increased the subject's popularity greatly. The real stars of the show are the haunted houses and places themselves, surrounded by 'reputation' and mystique which may or may not be deserved when it comes to hard facts.

After Sandwood Bay I had a 'bucket list' of haunted places I had to visit. These included the 'infamous' Ancient Ram Inn in Wooton under Edge, Gloucestershire. It was genuinely ancient, parts of it dated back to around the twelfth century; but no longer an Inn since 1968, when it was bought by the charmingly eccentric John Humphries. Long before such things could make substantial money, Humphries showed a genuine belief in the phenomena there, and encouraged 'experts' to stay. However, I must admit to braking investigative protocol by getting a good night's sleep on top of a bed in one of its most haunted chambers. The 'infamy' of the place had not appeared that night!

Over and above the 'B' list 'celebrity' places, there is a short and changeable 'A' list. Places that make claims to be possibly the most haunted of all. I made comment in the Preface about Harry Price calling his book on Borley Rectory *The Most Haunted House in England*, a tag that has stuck ever since. I am on friendly terms with the paranormal authors Eddie Brazil and Paul Adams who wrote an encyclopaedic book with Peter Underwood on the Rectory phenomena, and who inherited Underwood's artefacts from the Rectory — long since demolished after a fire. These included a quite impressive bell from the courtyard but also more trivial knick-knacks such as the wires of servants' bells and from memory, bits of bricks and curtain hooks. I would like to claim astonishment at the awe of fellow investigators when they occasionally reveal these small knick-knacks for others to hold — but secretly I will admit to being rather fascinated by such knick-knacks as well.

The quest for finding the 'most haunted' has obsessed ghost hunters since Victorian times, when it was perhaps Glamis Castle that gained Britain's first 'most haunted' reputation. This is the long-standing residency of the Bowes-Lyon family whose most famous member to date is undoubtedly Elizabeth Angela Marguerite Bowes-Lyon, the mother of our recently departed Queen Elizabeth II. As early as 1907 the author Charles Harper stated in his fascinating book with the unimaginative title of *Haunted Houses* that Glamis Castle is: 'Unquestionably the most famous haunted house in Britain'.

However, Harper also hints throughout his book that much of the phenomena may be mixed up with old legends.

This does not mean, of course, that houses haunted by reputation are not haunted by real life (or death?) spirits as well. When it comes to Glamis Castle, there does seem to be some basis in fact. The author, broadcaster and Ghost Club member James Wentworth Day (1899–1983) managed to get a 'golden ticket' to spend a week at the place. As well as observing the Grey Lady, one of the most active ghosts — he managed to record a temperature drop of no less than 10 degrees Fahrenheit lasting for 15 minutes at 2 a.m., before reverting to normal room temperature. Sadly, this was very much a one-off, as Glamis Castle is a now very tricky place to try to get permission to stay in.

What is clear is that to be the 'most haunted' you must be willing to enter both yourself and your property into the public glare. Public glare can come through high society Victorian chit chat, like that which surrounded the castle at Glamis, or more likely by way of the popular press these days. Either way, this can leave both owners and investigators open to accusations of having ulterior motives.

I would suggest that such an incentive is similar in any discipline that attempts to discover something new. Psychologists and scientists are far better established professions. Yet in such professions it is certainly not unheard of for some to overemphasize the results of their own piece of research.

Is red meat good or bad for you?

Does fracking cause damage to the environment?

These are questions that cause debate amongst qualified experts. Sometimes such experts are commissioned by interested parties and therefore potentially incentivised to stress points of experimentation and theory. Ghost hunting has this as well, without doubt, but it should not be judged any more harshly than any other discipline. A place called Chingle Hall near Preston, Lancashire, is a good example to test these arguments further.

In 1992 I found myself driving up to Chingle Hall with my colleague Annice Neville who I had met as part of the hypnotic regression team. We were not put off by the drive of well over 200 miles. After all, Chingle Hall had a huge reputation partly fuelled by its appearance on the popular TV series *Strange but True*; and at that time was being seriously reported as potentially the (new) most haunted house in England.

Chingle Hall dates back to 1260, built as the home of the Singleton family, and had a long-standing reputation for being haunted. It comes complete with a legend that one of the family, Eleanor Singleton, was kept captive in a room there from aged eight until her death at the age of twenty. The reputed phenomena seemed to increase after 1970 with the discovery of a priest hole. This is literally a hole for hiding priests who may have had a different religion to that which was allowed by the incumbent king or queen. After the discovery, Mrs Howarth, the owner of the house, saw, amongst other things, a figure of a woman in the Priests room, and a monk in the 'John Wall' room. She also heard unexplained footsteps and tapping on walls and furniture. It is interesting to note that most paranormal incidents seem to involve some kind of trigger. This can be the expectation of a past life during regression or even the sudden realisation that the house you lived in was a place of trauma.

It is possible that the finding of the priest hole may have brought back the quite macabre history of Chingle Hall to the front of the owner's mind. After all, John Wall, a Franciscan priest, was a resident prior to becoming a martyr for his religion when he was hanged, drawn, and quartered in 1689. It is rumoured that his head was buried in Chingle Hall grounds.

Whilst John Wall would have been an obvious candidate for any discarnate entity, the actual phenomena was of a general type. It was as if some strange power had been unleashed. Peter Underwood, for example, mentions a workman sandblasting the fireplace in the main hall suddenly running out screaming because he felt he was being watched. He also mentions 'visitors experiencing profuse bouts of sweating and even blackouts' (*Nights in Haunted Houses*, Underwood, 1994, p. 113).

A report from ASSAP, who investigated several times, also refers to Ms M.P. who started to sweat and cry when she heard strange noises around the house. Whether such extreme fear is just due to expectation of something within the fabric of a place is an interesting question which we will certainly return to later.

After Mrs Howarth's death, her sister lived there for a short while, but when she left it was empty for a few years, until in 1986 it was bought by John and Sandra Bruce. At this point, it was fair to say, that what was previously a friendly invitation for investigators became a more commercial venture — perhaps the first haunted house to hire itself out regularly for a commercial fee.

When Annice and I spent the night at Chingle Hall with five others on an ASSAP investigation, it is also fair to say that, despite expectations, we found the experience rather disappointing. Noises were at one point heard in the nearby apparently 'disused' barn, which is 'thought' to be haunted by the son of a former owner who hanged himself there, called

Longton. There was an initial reluctance by others to investigate the source. When later we did investigate, we found the likely source of the noises to be a rather friendly cow. Annice, in her excellent report pointed out that the commercial angle had perhaps just slightly stepped over the line noting that 'there was a notice requesting people to pay £5 for a spare Chingle Hall brick to save Chingle Hall. From what it was to be saved was not really specified'.

So Chingle Hall combines all the clichés of a reputedly haunted house, but for others has provoked apparent phenomena as well. It teaches valuable lessons in getting first sources which have not yet been followed up on. The source of the tale of poor Eleanor Singleton; the source of the tale of the Longton suicide would be useful to know.

When I first became Vice Chair (Investigations) of the Ghost Club in the late 1990s, I still had that urge for a 'big ticket' investigation. I looked to a place that been placed in the forefront of hauntings during the 1970s, Sandford Orcas Manor House in Dorset.

The house had been in the ownership of the Medlycott family since 1736 but was leased between 1967 and 1979 to a Colonel Francis Claridge. During Claridge's tenure, apparently, Claridge and his family experienced at least fourteen ghosts. Based on such extensive sightings Sandford Orcas gradually established its 'most haunted' claim. The number of ghosts is something I never take too seriously, as in an active case, each type of phenomenon can be given a 'personality' by those who experience them. Ghosts, though, do not normally tend to introduce themselves.

However, when I contacted the house as a possible prelude to an investigation in 1999, I was surprised when I got a full refutation of the events from Mervyn Medlycott. He stated that, even though he believed in the paranormal, nothing had been seen in the house for the 21 years since Claridge had left and none of the stories were known to the Medlycott family before.

These stories were very specific and included a young sea cadet, who was incarcerated in a room to avoid a public scandal, after committing a murder at sea. Note that Glamis also has a tale of incarceration as does Borley. The reported ghosts also included a seven-foot-tall footman who was jailed after accosting a girl from the village. If the stories were not known to the Medlycott family, I can think of no other explanation than that they were made up by the Claridges, possibly to boost attendances when the house was open for public visits.

This non investigation was a useful lesson in learning that a good 'haunting' or any spontaneous paranormal experience needs more than just publicity and reputation. It must also have a wide pool of witnesses to be relevant in an evidential sense. Some element of repeatability is surely the essence of what any science should be. It also reinforced the importance of finding original sources. In this case there was a near impossibility of the ghost story having a source since the historical owners knew of none. This meant, in all honesty, that all fourteen ghosts were most likely a work of fiction.

At this point I started to realise that for many, including myself, the romantic bias towards spending the night at a 'most haunted house' perhaps often gets in the way of the aim of getting to the actual truth of the matter. I gradually came to consider myself not as a 'ghost hunter' but simply a 'paranormal researcher'.

I have also found it can be just as interesting trying to unravel the experiences of others rather than hoping for that one rare experience of your own. After all, how can you look for trends when you are only 'studying' the experiences of one person — that one person being yourself?

I rather liked being able through logic to close the case of Sandford Orcas simply through finding out the facts through correspondence. It was also of great interest when I decided to do a little research into the previous case of the 'Silent Pool' in Shere that I had tried in my teenage years to make a 'documentary' about. As always, the key is to find the first source of the story. In this case the first source appears to not be from the annals of thirteenth-century history, but from a Victorian book by Martin F Tupper, *Stephan Langton or The Days of King John: A Romance of the Silent Pool* (1858).

This curiously long named book was written for several reasons. Its first purpose was as a tribute to Stephen Langton, who became Archbishop of Canterbury against the wishes of King John in 1207 and whose dispute with the king was an essential catalyst to the signing of England's first bill of rights, the Magna Carta, in 1215. By definition, Tupper was no fan of King John.

From the book's Introduction Tupper in addition admits he wanted to create 'interest in Albury and its Neighbourhood'. Albury being a village very close to the Silent Pool.

He also wished to 'clear my brain of numerous fancies and pictures'.

He did so by telling a tale of twenty historical characters to which he admitted the addition of some 15 additional fictional ones.

As there is no other first source for the drowning maid, I think we can safely assume that she is one of the fifteen characters invented by Tupper.

In effect, the ghost of the Silent Pool is a ghost story invented on a whim of colourful historical fiction to promote the wonderful countryside of Tupper's local area. Yet long after the fiction angle had been forgotten, the ghost angle lingers on.

I have picked on the Silent Pool simply because it attracted me so much in my earlier life. There are many other examples of romanticised fiction becoming discussed as fact. The famous haunted house at 10 Berkley Square, Mayfair, London, is another example. It likely got its reputation in Victorian times by its run-down appearance in a fashionable street when owned by a recluse. This was likely embellished by later writers such as Elliot O'Donnell.

The important point of showing the peculiar 'anatomy' of many ghost stories is simply to ask the question:

How can ghost hunting yet be a science when all too often what we are hunting is just a myth?

In between the all-out myths there are places like Chingle Hall that are a mix of myth and possible 'real' phenomena. The question I suspect that 'haunts' most respectable ghost hunters in a case such as that, is how to separate the 'wheat from the chaff', and to concentrate on the real things as opposed to the romantic legends. Much effort has been made to overcome this through the use of equipment both low and high tech.

In the Chingle Hall investigation every room came with thermometers and tape recorders provided by the other people in the group. The thermometers by themselves may have been a positive contribution so long as all investigators were aware that

1. Gradual cooling of the house was to be expected during the night. In the case of Chingle Hall it started cold and just got colder.
2. That a large temperature fluctuation can be a signal of many things. It is anecdotally connected with a haunting but there are few if any cases where the temperature drops at the point where a 'ghost' is seen. It is just as likely that the experience of seeing a ghost sends a cold chill down the witness's spine and makes them think the room is getting colder.

However, constant recording without any controls can be more of a hindrance than a help. In the case of Chingle there were seven investigators split into three groups. When listening to all those hours of tapes it would have been impossible to analyse whether a 'sigh' or a 'footstep' was coming from a group member, or whether a further 'uninvited guest' was providing some solid paranormal evidence. For such things to be useful, the groups must work together within specific protocol and comment verbally onto the tape if someone makes an unusual noise.

I am certainly not trying to be overcritical of my colleagues on this investigation. These are techniques that are used very frequently amongst the numerous groups of paranormal investigators that now exist both sides of the Atlantic. Post millennium, I have found the attitude to equipment has become more serious and the equipment used has become far higher tech. This though is sometimes to the point where the equipment itself becomes the sole point of the investigation, to the detriment of our eyes and ear and the testimony of others as well.

Even if I secretly thought of myself as a paranormal researcher at this point, I was also Vice Chair (Investigations) for the Ghost Club so I would feel obliged to spend a few more nights in romantic interesting places. In fact, I have never quite stopped but feel these days it must be less random and have a specific purpose towards what is trying to be proved.

Of my Ghost Club investigations three were to stand out for very different reasons indeed.

The first was when I hosted a group of investigators at the Clerkenwell House of Detention in 1999. A place that basically consisted of underground ancient cells turned into a combination of a chamber of horrors and a museum of nineteenth-century prison conditions. This was an interesting experience as my group of level-headed investigators picked up some very intense though subjective experiences. A non-psychic heard voices in his head from a condemned man, even though the Clerkenwell Prison had primarily been a prison for debtors and people on remand. A lady who claimed to be more psychic picked up the stench of burning flesh and others felt a presence. It seemed some of the investigators had been 'hypnotised' by the chamber of horrors effect and sensing what they would expect to see in such a strange place.

I am sure that at that point I could hear the (very much living) ghost of the friendlier sceptic Chris French in my head whispering 'Confirmation Bias'. The bias to interpretate evidence to one's existing beliefs — or in this case what one would believe to be in an underground prison and chamber of horrors.

The second case was when I hosted an investigation at Charlton House, a large old house dating back to the seventeenth century. The number of people exceeded a dozen which was fine for the venue but made it difficult for the controls that I would normally want. Inevitably, the investigation had to be split into groups.

Something very interesting did indeed happen that night. A wooden ornament in the shape of a mushroom (being used as a trigger object) flew off the table where it sat and onto the floor with a very loud crash — loud enough to be heard by the group next door. However, poor protocol meant that no one in that group had turned on a recording device. (Yes — the reader is quite right to notice that this error would have been unlikely to have happened with the 'over-organised' Chingle Hall group.) What we did have was a small group of people, some of whom did not know each other, witnessing the same thing. A wooden object crashing to the floor with a bang far louder than its weight would allow at face value cannot be a natural event. The presence of independent witnesses tends to lessen the likelihood of any sensible fraud scenario, so that incident still stood out as being positively 'evidential'.

The Final case I will briefly mention is a confidential one coordinated by myself and my colleague Rosie O'Carroll for the Ghost Club, where an unmarried mother in London had felt compelled to leave her modern social housing home because of an entity that physically pushed her, amongst other phenomena, and whose presence could be felt in a particular corner. She identified the entity as a tall dark male in his thirties. This case was interesting because neighbours corroborated that similar experiences had occurred to a different lady who had lived there previously and therefore potentially widened the witness pool. It was also a case where we subtly used mediums that corroborated most elements of the story without apparent prior knowledge, and a case where Rosie O'Carroll is positive that she heard footsteps on the stairs.

It is also a case that we could not complete, because after lobbying from ourselves and others, including the local MP, the lady and child got transferred to a different flat.

A fuller account of the above three cases can be read in my book on poltergeists.

I believe all these cases, so far, sum up a ghost hunter's dilemma perfectly:

1. When is a witness pool wide enough to take a case seriously or at least not treat it with the caution of a single witness case? (Note especially Sandford Orcas.)
2. The awareness we must all have of psychological explanations when it comes to ghosts and apparitions. (Note especially House of Detention.)
3. Where if ever we should use the apparently psychically gifted, and in what way. Not all psychically gifted people, after all, refer to themselves as being demonologists. (Note especially the council house haunting and House of Detention.)
4. Despite that urge to get to the truth of the matter, there are times, of course, when the needs of the witness of

possible paranormal phenomena must take precedence. (Note especially the council house case.)

5. Perhaps the biggest test of turning ghost hunting into a science is what equipment should be used, how and when it should be used, and especially how the evidence should be interpreted. (Note especially Chariton House and Chingle Hall.)

With regard to the final point, that of equipment use, I still remember the gradual change from low tech equipment to high tech equipment that came just after the millennium. I clearly remember being dragged out of bed to get my first EMF meter imported from the USA and the shocked, tired look in my eyes when I realised that import duty would have to be paid to the postman.

I also remember how cheap digital cameras made it so easy to suddenly study a picture on the spot. We got a good orb photo, for example, over a haunted fireplace while investigating Charlton House. This was only a temporary fascination as our photographic experts in the Ghost Club as well as the Society for Psychical Research gradually realised that the digital mechanism (especially in cheaper cameras) could cause orb-like blurs when dust or other particles were close to the lens. For those who still doubt this, ask yourself why spirits only started communicating in orb like fashion at the turn of the twenty-first century! In a later 'experiment' I conducted at a place called The Cage, St Osyth, I used what I wryly termed a 'magic broomstick'. Every time I swung the dusty magic broom Rosie O'Carroll was to confirm that 'Orbs' abounded on the digital video monitoring equipment. This was an experiment in the 'magic' of optical science, no less.

It is, I think, essential to remember that equipment measures the state of the environment, nothing more nothing less. The only good 'ghost detector' is an intelligent mind summing up the facts. That first EMF meter that I paid import tax on measures, not surprisingly, Electro Magnetic Frequency, an infrasound (low frequency sound) detector (much more specialist and expensive) measures exactly what it says. A Geiger counter as recommended by the paranormal investigator Joshua P. Warren in his book *How to Hunt Ghosts- a Practical Guide* (2009), measures radioactivity. However, should a Geiger counter start to register significantly, the only practical guidance I would give is to vacate that house very quickly!

The overall point being that equipment should be used selectively and the 'kitchen sink' should not be thrown into your investigation 'bag', which in some instances has literally become an investigators 'truck' these days.

Whilst I run into few decent ghost hunters that genuinely believe any equipment can detect a ghost, there is perhaps still a significant majority that believe certain changes in measurements might be at least an indicator of a possible ghostly presence. Whilst this has not been shown as untrue, it may in fact be the case that at least in some instances those ghost hunters are putting the cart before the horse as I will explain shortly.

What I hope the opening chapters have shown the reader (and myself when I had those experiences), is that when a person's frame of mind changes strange things start to occur. Most of those strange things so far have been in more pleasurable states of heightened consciousness. Be that through the inspiration of hypnosis, eating a Madeleine cake, or a cold meat pie in the ruins of Sandwood Cottage.

Not all changes of consciousness are pleasurable and one that many of us have experienced is those triggered by stress. Stress triggers the Amygdala or fear centre in the brain, production of the stress hormone cortisol, and shuts down parts of the conscious mind that are not needed for the 'flight or fight' response. It can, over a period, diminish the grey matter in the brain that is used for decision making and problem solving, while increasing the white matter used for communicating information.

To say then that stress in some way alters the state of a mind is obvious. As we will see in later chapters, it is often found to be a trigger for what seems to be a paranormal experience. Stress is normally seen as being triggered by personal circumstances but there is growing evidence that it can also be triggered by environmental factors as well.

With regard to power of Electromagnetism, T Balassa, R Szemerszky and Gy Bárdos (of the Department of Physiology and Neurobiology, Eötvös Loránd University, Budapest, Hungary) showed in their paper 'Effect of short-term 50 Hz electromagnetic field exposure on the behaviour of rats' (2009) that such exposure 'may influence behaviour, increase passivity and situational anxiety' (Abstract).

The level of exposure decided in this experiment was calculated to be the same level permitted by transformer stations located within buildings, so it was potentially a level a human could experience in real life.

Of great interest in general are the works of Michael Persinger, Professor of Psychology at Laurentian University, Canada. In particular, his paper 'Geopsychology and geopsychopathology: Mental processes and disorders associated with geochemical and geophysical factors' (1987).

Here Persinger states that 'geomagnetic [naturally occurring EMF] variations have been correlated with enhanced anxiety, sleep disturbances, altered moods'. He further notes that 'copper, aluminium, zinc, and lithium may influence the incidence of thought disorders ... [and that] these common elements are found in many soils and ground water'.

Water and the paranormal, as I was gradually to find, were something that often go hand in hand.

Infrasound is a little more problematic and also a little less frequent in the natural and manmade environment. It can be found in such things as severe weather, surf, avalanches, earthquakes, and volcanoes and waterfalls, none of which are common; while manmade sources include diesel engines, turbines, explosions, and some loudspeakers. In short, when infrasound is present the source should at least be more obvious. It can cause some unpleasant effects, including stress; particularly, it is thought, at a level of 18Hz. It can possibly even make windows rattle which would be a minor haunting/poltergeist experience naturally explained. But unlike electromagnetism whose natural and manmade sources are everywhere, it is more debatable as to how large an effect it could potentially have on so called haunted houses.

Some scientists have even suggested that black mould might also cause such sensations, but without any real evidence to back up this claim. In fact, the UK national paper the *Daily Mirror* contacted me more recently to discuss this possibility for an article that appeared under the frightening headline 'Black mould in your home can cause terrifying hallucinations of demons and ghosts'.

However, in an attempt to calm a frightened nation down, I told the *Daily Mirror* that

What happens from time to time is that 'academics' are keen to get a simple natural explanation to what is likely a complex event, be they 'paranormal' or not. There are far better theories for triggers that might momentarily change people's consciousness and give people the feeling of being totally 'spooked.'
(www.mirror.co.uk/news/uk-news/black-mould-your-home-can, 13 March,2019)

I feel that this is just a simplistic theory to try to find a natural explanation when their scientific paradigm can't.

So, when it comes to the use of equipment, I found the situation muddled and complex but as I was starting to discover there were elements of electromagnetism that could prove useful in the paranormal jigsaw I was trying to put together. It also seemed I was facing a paradox, in that at least some academics take ghost hunting seriously and treat it like a science, but yet it seemed most ghost hunters don't, using techniques and equipment in a random way. As I looked at my thickening lever arch files of case notes, there seemed only one way I could possibly contribute to set the record straight.

By trying to write a good book on the subject myself!

Such a book was presented to publishers as the first guide this side of the Atlantic instructing how to ghost hunt in the age of new equipment and television coverage. There had been two other guides I knew of in the past: *Ghost Hunting: A Practical Guide* by respected Investigator Andre Green (1973), which was followed up in 1986 by, not surprisingly, my old colleague Peter Underwood with *The Ghost Hunter's Guide*. By the early years of the millennium whilst both books still have sound advice they were, of course, rather dated in their approach. Some things never date, however, and I fully agree with a quote from Underwood's Publisher's book summary.

That to be a good ghost hunter 'you need to be part detective, part investigative reporter, a scientist, with a measure of the psychologist thrown in...'

The book I presented had a working title *The Strange Art of Ghost Hunting*. I tried at first the very best-known publishers that accepted work without an agent. Paradoxically, despite the subject's vast expansion in television media, it had become a specialist subject in book form. Despite my now quite 'official' sounding titles, former Vice Chair (Investigations) of the Ghost Club and subsequently Council member of the SPR, I quickly realised the need to concentrate on more specialist but still very respectable publishers.

The manuscript was accepted by the History Press, partially to complement the series of books they already had published on numerous haunted towns and regions. There was one proviso that the History Press was adamant about when it came to the book title, they simply didn't get the point I was making or the message I was trying to convey. The *Strange Art of Ghost Hunting* suddenly became *Ghost Hunting: A Survivor's Guide*, published in 2010.

So I slid the title in as this chapter's title after a delay of a mere 13 years and hope by now the reader is ready for the point I am trying to make!

After all, alchemy was equally a mysterious 'art', but somewhere along the way the alchemist Isaac Newton discovered a whole new paradigm of science.

Chapter 5

Poltergeists, the Missing Link?
(Can our noisy friend the Poltergeist start to fit the whole paranormal jigsaw together?)

A poltergeist can be defined as a ghost or other paranormal entity causing physical disturbances such as making loud banging noises and throwing objects about. Yet over the years their study has been neglected. In effect, they have been put in a specialist niche rather than being thought of as part of the same phenomenon. Even when they are put in the same 'box' the poltergeist is studied as if it is simply a ghost with attitude. I was starting to wonder if this could actually be the other way round.

Could it actually be that it is the 'attitude' that causes the 'ghost'?

I had not intended to cover time travel in this book but for the sake of showing how my thoughts on the paranormal started to fit into place, it is necessary to look back on things I may have experienced previously but only further reflected on in the light of more recent events. So this chapter, at least, jumps forward and backward a little with regard to the experiences I have had with the paranormal.

I remember attending the SPR conference in Leicester in 2019. This was one of the few recent occasions that I had gone to a conference without having a paper to present. It meant for a change that I could concentrating on listening to others.

One new speaker at the conference was Dr Urszula Wolski, Associate Lecturer of Psychology and Sociology at Buckinghamshire New University. The talk had an intriguing title, 'Researching the Researchers: An exploration into the experiences and beliefs of investigators of paranormal phenomenon', and I suddenly felt we were the ones under analysis rather than the paranormal 'entities' themselves. Wolski had through 'snowballing sampling', (a sampling technique where existing study subjects recruit future subjects from among their acquaintances), created data of the belief systems of those who were involved in paranormal research. Not surprisingly 12% were Pagans but more surprising the same percentage (12%) were atheists. A further 11% were, like me, agnostics while 20% had no religion at all. In short, 43% had no religious urge to believe there was 'anything more'.

When it came to what we researchers think, it becomes even stranger. Wolski's survey points out that even though 12% were atheists with an active disbelieve in God, only 1% had an active disbelief in paranormal phenomena. In effect, based on this survey, eleven out of twelve atheists, with a passing interest in our subject, look up to the sky and think in awe that it just might be possible there may be things that can only be explained outside of our current science.

I would be genuinely interested to know how both Richard Swinburne and Richard Dawkins would have viewed this survey, as it seems that so many people are inching forward in the quest for 'something else' without the necessity of the God or no God debate. However, if no God, then likely no evil demons for the demonologists to scare us with, likely no afterlife either, something has to, after all, maintain 'heaven' whatever that is. If no afterlife, where could discarnate spirits possibly fit in?

I was left reminded of what is, in effect, the 'ultimate' question. What possibly could the paranormal be?

That was a question that I started thinking about shortly after writing my ghost hunting book in 2010. Here I had decided as the last chapter makes clear, that ghost hunting whilst a romantic joy to participate in was not a 'science' as such. This was due in some part to the techniques used which I talked about in Chapter Four. It also seemed that so called 'discarnate' entities, with their apparent random actions, if existing at all were losing the essence of who they were.

To clarify that point my mind wandered back just a little further.

In my earlier days of investigating with the Ghost Club, in the late 1990s, I experimented a little with a Ouija Board. This was a legitimate experiment in my eyes simply to discover what caused the apparent process of communicating with another entity or world through a piece of 'innocent' polished wood and a planchette. I did take particular care not to use this equipment in somebody's private home, as the 'scare' factor of such an experiment can be close to that of interventions of our self-styled demonologist friends. This is an important point, as fear feeds stress, and both can cause symptoms of the paranormal, and both, of course, are unpleasant sensations which is not what we should be trying to achieve.

One such case of experimentation took place in a deserted house in a village near Ipswich. Here the only communication that made any sense was the one word 'Legions'. This appeared not to be meant as a reference to a Roman army but a quote from the Bible, 'my name is Legion, for we are many', made by two demons possessing a man (Matthew, 8:28–34, and other New Testament sources).

It is a slightly garbled message even from the biblical source and far more so with the one-word answer that we got. Surely, a demon, spirit or any intelligent being would do better than that?

Another Ouija Board session was in the haunted basement of a famous insurance company. During this session a communicator claiming to be from the nineteenth century gave more information this time. It claimed to be the wife of Reginald Fox who lived in Hatfield and named the street they lived in. No street of that name existed in Hatfield, nor any record of Reginald Fox. Exactly as if under hypnosis, one or more of our subconscious minds seemed to be giving us what we wanted in a rather dull records basement.

These experiences started to make more sense when I later read of the Andover Case which took place in 1974, and which was investigated by a much younger version of my colleague Barry Colvin, still a member of the SPR council to this day.

This case involved poltergeist disturbances which happened to the Andrews family in a modern council house, built in the 1960s in Andover, Hampshire, UK. Much of the phenomena seemed to consist of rapping sounds coming from the wall in one of the bedrooms and the catalyst for the phenomena seemed to be 12-year-old Theresa Andrews. When Colvin investigated, the sounds started to communicate in a laborious way by tapping through the alphabet to the desired letter. Through this system the 'entity' identified 'himself' as a gentleman called Eric Waters. However, the 'profound' messages that Eric had to give the non-spiritual world consisted to a large extent of simply trying to predict the following week's soccer results. This he managed to do without any degree of accuracy above chance.

In the same case, a local spiritualist added that there was a young boy buried in the cellar. Apart from the fact that Eric claimed to be a man rather than a boy, this is as big a cliché as the common re-incarnation claim to having a past life as Napoleon. It is in fact a direct hash of the famous nineteenth-century Fox sisters' case in the USA when a pedlar was claimed to be buried in the cellar. A case that led to the rise of the spiritualist movement itself and to which our spiritualist would have likely been fully aware.

So, I discovered from this case using the afterlife theory that the 'lost soul' of Eric Waters and (possibly) a lost soul of a murdered young boy simply wanted to predict the football results!

The overall point I was finding is that if discarnate spirits were causing such things, these discarnates were, in effect, the equivalent of the 'bar room bore' — coming out with random, meaningless comments before descending back into incoherent inebriation. Surely, a far easier explanation in the Andover case is that the communications in fact came from the subconscious mind of a 12-year-old adolescent girl with a liking for football. Anything else would be doing 'spirits' from the afterlife a stunning 'disservice'.

I was fascinated by one very big difference between the trivial communications from the Andover Case and the trivial Ghost Club communications.

The Ghost Club communications involved our collective fingers on a planchette, and the likely cause was no less than what the famous scientist Michael Faraday (1791–1867) had called the automatic theory. This postulates that the Ouija Board is moved (assuming no fraud) by subconscious muscle spasms of one or more of the operators. My experience of being on the board seemed to confirm this. It felt similar to when I was in shallow trance hypnosis, and I could nearly feel my fingers starting to urge it, if it was not being pushed already. This also can fit comfortably into everyday science.

Andover, however, had disembodied raps when Colvin was in sight of the people in the room. If fraud could be discounted, something outside every day science was certainly happening — something most would refer to as paranormal!

At that point I started to remember all those places I had previously investigated and how so many of them just had phenomena based on legends, 'White Ladies' or 'Black Monks' that were rarely if ever seen. Of the cases that had been active to a point such as Chingle Hall (though not on our visit), any sightings seemed to go hand in hand with rapping on furniture or the perceived sounds of footsteps (which could in fact be rapping on the floor). Others had movement of objects such as the fire doors flying open and trigger objects being moved, such as when a figure was seen by some of the group who investigated RAF Cosworth.

The two phenomena seem to go together as if there was an energy that triggers a noise or a movement and then that energy is seen. When we talk of the ghosts of these 'White Ladies' and 'Black Monks' (etc.), most apparitions are mainly flimsy changes of light patterns which people deem to have taken a human form.

So, it seemed to me possible that any apparitional sightings might simply be residual energy from poltergeist phenomena, and yet up till now they were often discussed as being two very different things.

As, by then, I claimed to be a 'paranormal researcher', some research was required on the opinions of others regarding these ideas. By far the most encyclopaedic effort on poltergeist phenomena that I discovered was *Poltergeists* (1979) by SPR members Alan Gauld and Tony Cornell. This book was a historical analysis of 500 cases old and new; it showed that 29% of poltergeist cases had visual apparitions and a similar amount of audio/voice like phenomena. This they termed 'Intermediate Cases' where the phenomena of (apparently) different categories is combined. Now poltergeist cases unlike 'romantic' apparitions are in the main well authenticated phenomena. Unlike apparitions there is no question as to whether they are simply a trick of the light. If there is an unnatural door movement, if an object is thrown, if an audible bang is heard, chances are there is something well worth investigating. There may be a natural explanation but in more robust cases such as Enfield, it would, I believe, be reduced to two logical scenarios — either something paranormal or fraud. I couldn't think of many regular apparitions appearing without the poltergeist bits added as well, though, as Gauld and Cornell point out there are plenty the other way round.

I was left wondering if 'apparitions' are simply a poltergeist 'side effect'.

A few years ago, the next part of the jigsaw literally landed on my door. The wife of a couple that I know was having a clear out of old papers from the attic which included a few journals, some of which were old SPR ones. She gave me these as a gift. I gathered the ones in good condition and opened one of them on a random page. Finding a well-researched article written by G. W. Lambert, 'Poltergeists: A physical theory' (1955). Here Lambert found 54 poltergeist cases with verifiable locations and found that nearly 50% had taken place within three miles of tidal water. He took 33 of these where the month was specified and found that 27 of them took place in the wetter winter half of the year. I am unsure whether those facts or the way I found them was most compelling to me. They were, however, evidence that poltergeists and water seem to possibly be in some unknown way linked.

I was thinking how important it would be to try to do some similar work in the long term on areas of high geomagnetic activity. I am not aware of any that has been done — but if the reader wishes to correct me on this, please do? There are certainly interesting cases associated with electromagnetic and geomagnetic issues. A group called Parascience, which sometimes works closely with the SPR, investigated a case in a Welsh farmhouse in 2003. There was a particular part of this farmhouse in which phenomena was prone to happen including the appearance of colourful lights that have the potential to be misinterpreted as visual apparitions. Also included were more conventional types of poltergeist activity such as cupboard doors opening, and small toys being thrown.

The Parascience team were to discover two very interesting things:

1. that a natural geological fault line went beneath the house to a level of up to 1,800 metres, and
2. that the electrical cables just outside the windows were in a very poor state and were emitting EMF to a very high level.

In effect, Parascience had discovered a case that included both natural geomagnetic and manmade electromagnetic sources of energy that could potentially be the trigger.

More recently, I was contacted about a similar sounding case. Here I was in detailed correspondence with the lady who reported the disturbances. Unfortunately (from a research point of view) the lady and her partner thought carefully about a full investigation but politely declined in the end as they were shortly to move out of the house. I will therefore, of course, for the sake of confidentiality, just talk of this report in the most general of terms. I found this an intriguing case because of the following factors:

1. The lady admitted without any prompting that she was very sensitive to electrical energy, got spontaneous electrical shocks and felt sick in places with fluorescent lights.
2. She stated that the energy she felt seemed to peak during the winter. This I found fascinating based on Lambert's Survey.
3. A particular bout of phenomena began with her feeling lightheaded. She then had a feeling of being gently pushed, in common with many poltergeist cases. She also reported an inexplicable sound of a choir of voices in the vicinity and also felt she was seeing something through the corner of her eye. Potentially, a perfect example of what Gauld and Cornell would have termed an 'Intermediate Case'. Visual sparks of electricity were also observed.

4. The lady also stated to having grown up in a different house where other phenomena had taken place. She recollected that it was in the vicinity of a large electrical pylon in the field across the road.

5. The lady thought she felt energy coming from people and could read them. Which I personally find as a near perfect description of being to some extent psychic.

6. There was also an ancient earth mound close to her house. This, as I was to discover, could also be a relevant factor in paranormal incidents.

It is a great shame, I think, that cases like this can't be fully investigated. They are cases that have potentially most of the environmental connections to the jigsaw of what constitutes paranormal phenomena. Cases, however, are not just cases; they are people having strange experiences. Our thirst for knowledge should never come before the thirst for others to lead a quiet and peaceful life.

Whilst this case had most of the environmental connections, without further investigation it was impossible for me to say if it had the 'other' triggers that seemed to be common. In Chapter Four I mentioned the growing possibility in my head that both negative as well as positive changes in our states of minds could lead to strange incidents. In effect, negative energies triggered by environmental effects. Of course, arguably, even more bouts of 'negative energy' are triggered by more personal events. Such events, I was thinking, could, of course, include adolescence. This is several years of 'stress' for many and often a major catalyst in any poltergeist case. It seemed to me likely that such incidents are not caused by 'adolescence' itself, as so many cases have other stress related triggers.

Such triggers are fully discussed in my book *Poltergeists: A New Investigation into Destructive Hauntings*, but to just give a small flavour by taking some cases mentioned in my previous book, I would include:

Case	Location & Approximate Timeline	Possible Trigger Causes
Enfield Poltergeist	Late 1970s. Enfield, London	Adolescence/ Illness in family
Black Monk Pontefract	Began late 1960s. Pontefract, Yorkshire, UK	Adolescence/ Family tension
Kern City Poltergeist	1981–2. Kern City, Bakersfield, California	House move/ Recent death
Amityville Horror	1975–76. Amityville, Long Island, New York	House move/ Financial pressures/Recent deaths
Gef, the Talking Mongoose	Early 1930s. Dalby, Isle of Man	Adolescence/ Loneliness
Langenhoe Church	1930s–1950s. Langenhoe, Essex, UK	Fault line (previous earthquake)
Rosenheim Poltergeist	Late 1960s. A lawyer's office in Rosenheim, Germany	Marriage engagement broken
Bell Witch (Poltergeist?)	1817. Tennessee, USA	Argument over land purchase/ Recent death

Of particular interest were the factors of 'recent deaths and 'house move'. The reason for this being that it would be all too easy to attribute the cause of the poltergeist to the dead person in the case of the former. In the case of the latter, the perception would be from the person who moved house that the house itself was haunted, when possibly the stress of the house move had 'haunted' the house.

The case of the Kern City poltergeist, I believe, makes a great example of these two factors. The poltergeist 'victim' in this case being a lady called Frances Freeborn who in 1981, at the age of 63, moved into a housing retirement community (Kern City). She moved there alone, so most definitely excluding any adolescence factor. The premises she moved into remained fully furnished to the style of a single lady who had died a few years previously, so the house would have been a constant reminder of the former owner's 'presence'.

I in no way wholly discount the possibility that the spirit of the previous lady caused doors to swing, drawers to be opened and pictures to be removed. This indeed was the theory of experienced investigator Dr Stafford Betty who investigated the case and published it in the SPR Journal. However, the spirit of the lady would have had ample opportunity to voice her objections when two mediums visited, and all the mediums could pick up was the 'presence' of an elderly couple and a younger lady.

I found, yet again, a case of a poltergeist saying nothing of sense and certainly not behaving like a mature lady should by passing on a meaningful message to Freeborn.

If the afterlife is the cause of a poltergeist, why are there so many cases where the death of another seemed not to be an obvious factor, and where there were consistently other immediate factors and causes that appeared to act as a trigger?

Why would, for example, phenomena simply happen in an ordinary law office in Rosenheim, Germany, were it not for the fact that the broken engagement of Anna Marie Schnabel led her to subconsciously discovering hidden powers in her mind to vent her obvious frustration?

When a theory appears to fit many of the facts, surely it is the job of professional scientists to, at the very least, test out its validity? This may happen in time, but with no scientific clamour at present it is still left to the largely amateur paranormal researcher — with constraints in time, funding, equipment and if a researcher is being honest, constraints in some specialist knowledge in certain areas as well.

I mentioned earlier how essential I feel it is, especially when it comes to active cases in private residences, that a researcher's quest for truth should never come before the need of the residents to lead a quiet and peaceful life. Unfortunately for Vanessa Mitchell, owner of a residential property in St Osyth, Essex, known as The Cage any attempt at having a 'quiet life' ceased for nearly a decade after 2010.

The Cage, St Osyth, was not a made-up name. It was embedded on a local history plaque on the house that was formerly used as a holding cell. This plaque also stated that the witch Ursula Kemp was imprisoned there (apparently with eleven of her followers) before she was hanged at nearby Chelmsford. From the size of the cell room you can only imagine the depth of despair that caused. The house was also the site of a more recent suicide. Such factors like this are like the stress factors that were present in the infamous Amityville Case in Long Island, USA, in that the house in Amityville was genuinely the site of mass murder. It seems likely that a house move under such circumstances will cause a certain amount of anticipation and stress.

Initially, Ms Mitchell lived there with friends but ended up there alone with her young child. Events were to unfold that included apparitions, including a historical type of old lady but also a man dressed in modern day clothes. Of interest to note is that apart from well-formed apparitions, Ms Mitchell and a witness also saw floating lights in the lounge which seemed to me like the electrical charges I mentioned in previous cases. This happened along with poltergeist incidents such as Ms Mitchell being pushed by an unseen hand and a can of coke sliding mysteriously across a table, as well as some very interesting JOTT type events. Ms Mitchell also stated that her moods started to alter, and she entered a state of what she has termed depression.

I should say at this point that Vanessa Mitchell believed her house to be haunted in the conventional sense, though by whom or what was never quite clear. This was not helped by other visitors who produced paranormal photos which were in some cases pareidolia (the tendency to perceive a specific, often meaningful image in an ambiguous visual pattern). In other cases, photographs were possibly faked. The best/worst case of likely pareidolia was a 'demonic goat' that got into the national newspapers which on visual analysis was likely the fur hood of a coat taken in the pitch dark turned sideways. It did, however, produce possibly the best 'worst' headline in the online version of the Daily Star: 'Who are you gonna call? Goat busters!' (31 Jan 2016).

Vanessa Mitchell had reported the case to the SPR in 2010. She kept in touch with me afterwards, and was open to further investigation. Meanwhile the case had hit the headlines and was ultimately to be the subject of a fairly authentic docudrama *The Witches' Prison* (2018), starring Michelle Ryan (previously of the well-known UK soap opera *Eastenders* and of *Wonder Woman* fame in the USA). In effect, The Cage was for a time hitting the 'most haunted' category of house that I referred to in Chapter Four.

For a paranormal research body, the SPR is thankfully relatively well funded and can give out reasonably generous grants through two sources. The first is the General Psi Research Fund through which funds are normally given for academic studies. The second of these funds is the Survival Research Fund, which supports scientific research into the fundamental question of whether some aspect of consciousness or personality survives bodily death. I personally wish there was a third fund for field research which would help bring what most paranormal researchers do (i.e., looking for evidence in the places that apparently have evidence) far closer to working in some form of academic way. As currently this option does not exist, I decided that the Survival Research Fund was the most suitable to approach. Whilst I do not instinctively favour a survival explanation, I do not discount it and conduct any research with an open mind. After some follow up questions, I obtained the funds I was seeking to hopefully investigate every angle of this intriguing haunting.

The purpose of this research was initially two-fold. The primary reason was to test out the depth of witness testimony. To see how far it extended beyond the experiences of Vanessa Mitchell and see if it could in some way be compared to the most famous cases previously on record such as Borley Rectory and Enfield. This is what at this stage I considered to be my expertise. There had also initially been a secondary purpose to invite equipment experts into the house to look for any triggers that might come from the environment as well. Unfortunately, those I had in mind were not available at the time which was a bigger loss than I first realised considering the type of witness testimony I was to get. With the paranormal there are always a few pieces of that complex jigsaw that are still left to complete.

My colleague Rosie O'Carroll and I were to be given free access to The Cage over the period of a few days. We decided that simply staying there for that period was unlikely to achieve much apart from possibly spooking ourselves. The place after all had been thoroughly investigated in that ad hoc way by others. It was also not a place where people who had experienced things could be interviewed at their ease. So whilst we spent a significant amount of time at The Cage, we took advantage of the fact that St Osyth is in fact a seasonal tourist village surrounded by caravan parks, and, in effect, set up what we half-jokingly called an 'SPR' outpost in a deluxe 6-berth trailer unit just outside the village. Here we could interview witnesses at their ease over cups of tea in the lounge without the 'awkwardness' of being at The Cage.

With regard to our time spent at The Cage, it is fair to say we were not overrun by spirits or other phenomena. In fact, we further rationalised the photographic evidence by way of creating orbs on video cameras by waving what we called the magic broom as I mentioned in Chapter 4. We also had a close look at items dug up in previous amateur excavations that were indicative of the house being situated on an ancient site. However, nothing paranormal happened during the time we spent at The Cage. This was not unexpected; I have always thought about the paranormal as being like fishing — not getting a catch doesn't mean that there are no fish in the river. It was also not our prime purpose of being there.

During the time of our stay we interviewed various key witnesses in the comfort of the caravan looking for consistency in the stories and experiences without, of course, asking leading questions. This was followed up by both telephone interview and email correspondence with others who had experienced things but did not live nearby, as the place had been independently investigated by other groups. By the end of this project I was fascinated by the fact that there did appear to be a good degree of consistency in the type of experience encountered. This included particular doors slamming closed without any particular reason, some positive EMF readings (but using only basic equipment) and people getting the feeling of being 'pushed' around the area of the stairs.

The two most dramatic consistent events were of people nearly passing out and becoming hysterical in The Cage and also at least five incidents of unexplained scratches or marks appearing on people's skin. The former event is best summed up by a quote from experienced Danish investigator Kim Sondergaard: 'I started to feel as if my legs would not carry me … I bumped into the wall … I suddenly felt a strong hatred … then I broke down … I started to cry uncontrollably.'

Whilst we might have some psychological explanation for some of these extreme emotional events, we cannot put such an explanation on the actual physical events. What interested me is the fact that something had caused the mind such stress — over and above that expected in the average 'haunted' house. Which is why it was perhaps so disappointing that we did not have environmental experts to seek a possible cause.

A further strange thing about The Cage is the long-standing plaque on the outside wall that states that it was used in the sixteenth century for holding witches. The history of village lockups (places to temporarily hold wrongdoers until they can be dealt with through the legal system) shows those that still exist are basically eighteenth- and nineteenth-century buildings. In fact, there is debate as to whether The Cage even appears on an early nineteenth-century map. My theory is that the plaque was added in the 1970s when the lock-up was converted as part of a house and mixed up the real witch incidents in St Osyth with a much newer building. So there were likely never witches at The Cage, but it seems that a combination of the story and other as yet unproven factors seem to trigger something within us and ensure 'the power of a witch' is let loose.

This is not a novel theory from me in my aim to fit everything neatly into one paranormal box. As early as 1972 the Toronto Society for Paranormal Research (TSPR) discussed and meditated on a totally fictional seventeenth-century Cavalier whom they called Philip. They gradually got Philip to communicate through poltergeist raps and move objects just like any self-respecting poltergeist should. This experiment has similarities to the concept of thought forms or 'Tulpas' which is something that is common in the mysticism of such Eastern countries as Tibet. Such ideas were once more widely put forward in the west as well, especially by theosophist and political campaigner Annie Besant, through her 1901 book *Thought-Forms*. Such ideas though seem to, all too easily, be put to one side as they do not fit our 'romantic' need for afterlife ghost stories.

My romantic 'right brain' still is 'haunted' by the notion of the spirit 'Emma', the drowned girl in the Silent Pool. However, I am no longer fourteen and my left brain knows it simply doesn't fit the facts.

So when it comes to the paranormal, could we possibly say that we actually haunt ourselves?

I noted at the start of this chapter that we would be indulging in a touch of time travel to past events, to explain how my thoughts on the paranormal were gradually forming. In most good time travel stories, you end up back in the present day and at the point of writing (June 2022) I was yesterday at a very convivial Ghost Club meeting where the speaker, Claire O'Malley, was discussing the (romantic?) passion she had for the subject of haunted cemeteries. Indeed 'Tombstone Tourism' is a popular interest which overlaps the paranormal. Such key 'A-List' places of interest includes The Merry Cemetery in Săpânța, Romania, with mainly happy bright caricatures of all the residents buried there. Other places such as the Chase Vault in Barbados have a more supernatural twist because until it was emptied, the coffins appeared to move even when the vault was locked.

However, it was Claire's tale of the poltergeist of Greyfriars Cemetery in Edinburgh that interested me most. This had perhaps gone under my radar over the years due to the cemetery's likely romanticised nineteenth-century association with Greyfriars Bobby a dog who apparently sat by his master's grave for fourteen years after his master's death. A dog that subsequently had a novel written about him in 1902 and a Disney film in 1961. In fact cemetery dogs fed by curators and visitors were common in such times and may have given the good Edinburgh folk the wrong impression as to why 'faithful' Bobby was there.

This has perhaps partly obscured a far more interesting story, that of the Mackenzie poltergeist which mainly 'haunts' the mausoleum of Sir George Mackenzie, the former Lord Advocate of Scotland who in 1679 was responsible for the torture and death of hundreds of (Presbyterian) covenanters. Undoubtedly, Mackenzie was an unpleasant man who would not have appreciated the accidental desecration of his monument in 1998 when a vagrant broke into it and subsequently fell into a plague pit below.

The mausoleum long had a history of being haunted; it was mentioned as being so by the famous author Robert Louis Stevenson as early as 1890. As I have previously discovered, many places have such enchanting legends that when re-awaked, seem to prime us for real-life inexplicable experiences. After the experience of this vagrant, people who toured the mausoleum were to start fainting or getting into a state of hysterical panic. Equally common was strange bruising and scratching that appeared during visits.

At this point in the Ghost Club meeting even our cool-headed Chair, Barrister Alan Murdie, was to intervene and explain that while not unnerved in the Mackenzie Mausoleum he had found himself inexplicably bruised the next day.

I later read an interesting book which was written on the phenomena as early as 2001 by Jan-Andrew Henderson who, like me, had taken down a great deal of witness testimony. He also found consistencies such as the phenomena being more likely to occur near the mausoleum entrance, although some even occurred in the apartments next to the mausoleum. The similarity to my study of phenomena at The Cage seemed obvious, but with far more visitors those affected run into the hundreds and continue to this day.

As Henderson puts it in page 10 of his book: 'There may be a scientific explanation for this phenomenon ... maybe scientists aren't trying hard enough.' Perhaps they don't believe enough to really explore. Henderson also quoted my 'old friend' Robert M. Pirsig from his unique book *Zen and the Art of Motorcycle Maintenance*. The quote begins: 'Laws of nature are just human inventions like ghosts ... the world has no existence outside the human imagination.'

So Pirsig the sceptic has (perhaps) inadvertently stated that the paranormal comes from within us but as the concept of science does as well, why then are they treated so unequally?

The title of Henderson's book sums my up present-day views on poltergeists perfectly:

The Ghost That Haunted Itself!

Chapter 6

Unlocking the Mind during Lockdown
(Exploring the ideas of others when little else can be explored)

You find your face scowling
at the taste of harsh instant coffee
sipped during 'countryside walks'.
Twelve steps to the back garden fence ... twelve steps back to the
kitchen door.
The option of extra sugar but the taste is still bittersweet,
the taste of options closing
like the doors of the boarded-up coffee shops.
[In the fully locked up for Non-Essentials High Street.]

In 2020, for the first time in several decades, I tried writing poetry again — the quote from the above effort being titled 'The Nespresso Machine in the Attic'.

I found such things a necessity to keep the mind alive when faced with possibly the biggest case of mass hysteria since the English Civil War of the seventeenth century. A time of real uncertainty that had been blighted by the hysteria of witch trials. These were done largely on a 'for profit' basis by the infamous 'Witch Finder General' Matthew Hopkins. Such hysteria often emerges during a crisis and was likely also the cause of the imprisonment of Ursula Kemp and her colleagues at St Osyth.

Like the Civil War, COVID-19 was a very real threat and I still occasionally choose to wear a mask to this day. However, as the whole thrust of this book is about the power of the mind, I will to this day object to the slow strangulation of the human spirit that long-term lockdowns brought in the UK and so much of the world.

The poem as it happened seemed to raise the spirits of some in the Nestle Corporation to which I sent it on a whim, and maybe some on the local online paper, *InsideCroydon.com*, in which it was published.

Other novel ideas included a 'Cocktail Tree' which grew 'magically' in that small back garden. In fact a bush with empty cans of instant cocktails attached. It is at times like this that you are most happy that there is someone to share such a unique 'trial' with, a good time to mention that I had married in 2003.

It didn't help my mood when just after lockdown began, I learnt in April 2020 that my old childhood 'hero' the goalkeeper Peter Bonetti had died. Whilst great on his day he had become (in)famous for a fumble on a rare appearance for the England team that may have put them out of the 1970 World Cup. He had subsequently finished his career outside the English elite league at clubs such as St Louis Stars (USA) and Dundee United (Scotland). It suddenly seemed that even men with inexplicable 'powers' and skills could be all too human at times.

Things had seemed so different the previous year when despite another sad death possibilities and thoughts were certainly starting to become a good bit clearer. An above average year filled with optimism and plans.

In February 2019 I had learnt of the acceptance of my book on poltergeists for the next year. This was celebrated at Joe's Bar, a unique place (yes — run by a man called Joe). The bar specialised in drinks with their special 'home brewed' mixers. Since lockdown, the place became boarded up just like the poem.

In April 2019 I was invited to and attended the funeral of a gentleman by the name of David Farrant. Farrant was an intriguing character that I had got to know fairly well. Of particular interest to me was that he was one of the key initial primary sources of information with regard to the haunting of Highgate Cemetery by an alleged vampire — one of the cases that had so many years back prompted me to try to make a 'young filmmakers' documentary. Farrant had lived a colourful life in and out of the national press but claimed he had little belief in the vampire tale. He believed his experiences and those of others, in spotting the figure of a tall man, were simply sightings of a ghost. Of further interest to my theories on the power of electromagnetism is the fact that there is a large radio/TV tower in Swains Lane, just outside the cemetery where the ghost/vampire was seen. Of further interest to those who have 'romantic' notions of connections and meaning, this TV tower stands fairly close to the grave of Michael Faraday (1791–1867). Faraday, of course, made such large contributions to our understanding of electro-magnetic effects.

In September 2019 I presented a talk on my forthcoming book at the ASSAP conference in Bath. I also enjoyed the SPR conference in Leicester later that month. For once I had no talks to give or responsibilities. I visited the grave of Richard III who had recently been buried with dignity in Leicester Cathedral. His remains had been found there recently, under parking space number *three* in the municipal parking lot. Another of those romantic coincidences that makes a paranormal investigator wonder if there is hidden meaning in the world.

By October 2019 some presales copies of my book had arrived which I would sometimes sell to colleagues and potential reviewers prior to the launch next year. In these modern times of PayPal, I was pleasantly surprised when I received 'real' money through the post, from the author Darren Ritson, best known for the 'South Shields' poltergeist case. This was hidden, I assume for safe keeping, inside a blank unsigned birthday card. By a wonderful bit of synchronicity, however, it arrived on my birthday — my first 'birthday card money' since my aunts and uncles did similar when I was a child. A big thanks to Mr Ritson — does anyone know when his birthday is by chance?

The year 2020 began in a similar way with those far away reports in China of apartment doors being welded shut due to a strange new virus being largely ignored in Europe. Such things could never happen in the 'Liberal West' of course!

In early January 2020 my curiosity got the better of me and I attended an in-depth talk on the 'Magick' of the occultist Alistair Crowley (1875–1947). A controversial figure deemed by some national papers of the time to be the 'The Wickedest Man in the World'. Yet Crowley was also a man of talent and will. He was an accomplished mountaineer and one of the first Westerners to attempt to climb K2 in 1902. His climb apparently reached a height of 6,525 metres not surpassed till 1938. He was also a prolific novelist, playwright, poet, and painter.

Magic (or Magick as Crowley termed it) be it 'white' or 'black' normally treads its own separate path from other aspects of the (slightly) more 'respectable' paranormal. Following the writing of my poltergeist book and the clear connections the poltergeist phenomena had with other types of the 'paranormal', I was curious as to how far this connection could go.

In January 2020 I visited Paris with my wife and met with the delightful Sandy Lakdar, formerly of the well-known TV series *Help! My House Is Haunted*. Here I was interviewed in an equally delightful atmospheric central Paris Chateau to help complete her documentary *For the Love of Ghosts* — an exploration into the unique attitudes the British have on the paranormal. We were both unaware at that point that this intriguing documentary, like most other things, was in danger of being suspended in time.

While in Paris we also met with a nephew who was studying there. He mentioned that there had been a report of that strange virus in the suburbs earlier that week. We felt momentarily intrigued but continued our lunch in a popular café overflowing with fellow diners.

In February 2020 I received interesting reports of a battery throwing poltergeist. I was going to visit the people's home until initially thwarted by a hurricane that took place on the day of the planned visit. I put it in my diary as a possible follow-up in the coming weeks! I was also happy to give a February talk to the SPR based on my Poltergeist book, selling some advanced 'review' copies. As is the SPR tradition, I was invited to dinner as the speaker by SPR Council Member Graham Kidd. I politely 'rebelled' pointing out that the dinner allowance would be better spent with all the audience who cared to walk over to the bar across the road. I believe a good time was had by all including Mr Kidd himself.

In early March 2020 there was an indirect contact with COVID-19 at my office with slight encouragement to work from home. This did not stop me visiting France again where my in-laws reside in a delightful village near Bordeaux. Here apart from visiting the local restaurants and bars, I spent time enjoying the spring weather on the patio and preparing a talk for the Ghost Club shortly after I returned. My understanding of French is still sadly limited, so I only had vague grasps of news reports that talked of parts of Italy locking down.

I returned to UK to an email from the Ghost Club asking if 'under the circumstances' I was still happy to speak, I said I was more than happy to do so. However, just a few days from the talk my life and the lives of others were suddenly put on hold!

I did not keep a diary at that time, but my pre-COVID-19 year seems so clear and gives the reader a grasp as to what a paranormal year in my life entailed at that point. My COVID-19 experiences are by contrast fuzzy and indefinable. I am sure Colin Wilson or even Gurdjieff would have summed it up by saying that the whole of a nation was living in a 'waking sleep'.

Yes, we did find a Nespresso machine in the attic which was dusted down and frequently used. We did buy an exercise bike which I believe we used for a few weeks. I did finally give that talk to the Ghost Club but over the impersonal media of Zoom, but I certainly was not inclined to rebel and to ask the audience into a 'virtual' pub.

I tried walking to local parks but got little from passing other half-asleep people in the same state as me. As the days and weeks passed, I discovered new places that would more suit an explorer of the paranormal. These included Queens Road Cemetery, just a short walk away from my home. Though it might not have been as grand or nearly as large as Highgate, it did come complete with disused chapel and Gothic arch and few other visitors, and a nice oval shaped walk with benches even the most draconian jobsworth wouldn't dare put a 'do not use' sign on. Sometimes, I would walk with coffee or something else in a flask — only, of course, to be drunk if the need was fully essential and therefore in line with the strange new COVID-19 restrictions. I decided to use these times to clear the mind in this unique place and come up with new ideas.

The first thing I decided was that the scientific process was perhaps as political as the politics I had been involved in, which perhaps is the reason that the paranormal has been excluded from even the most basic experimentation.

Do scientists have too much intellectual investment in existing beliefs to even consider their possible incompleteness?

I watched, as the pandemic continued, how government scientific experts in the UK would claim that masks could do no good in the middle of a shortage of masks, and even worse that you had to be 'experts' to put the damned thing on. Then this advice strangely changed as soon as the shortage was over. This is not a book for 'unmasking' the long-run masking debate, but those pieces of cloth have been around since the turn of the century and used in the Spanish Flu pandemic and yet still science has no consensus? I was even more shocked to read that there was still a debate going as to whether similar viruses were spread by droplets or aerosol spray from breath.

If this was the state of Science of Epidemiology (the study of control of diseases) could science even be trusted with tackling what we currently call paranormal phenomena?

At this point a squirrel might venture out from behind a tree in the cemetery — as if to give a shy and tacit approval of my thoughts.

As my frustration of mainstream science subsided, I started to think more of the paranormal itself — with those walks under that Gothic arch in the graveyard far more inspiring than the twelve steps I wrote about earlier to the end of my garden fence. I remembered that lecture on Crowley and remembered those UFO cases others had studied that I had ignored as perhaps outside my own agenda.

Perhaps, similar to those COVID-19 scientists, I also had too much investment in a traditional ghost and poltergeist agenda to seriously consider its incompleteness to date?

Whatever your views are on the large multinational called Amazon, its book delivery service was my only associate in further research — arriving mostly by unseen hands — just a knock on the door and the sound of a car or van driving away. Delivering little pieces of 'magic' (or 'Magick' according to Crowley) in paperback or occasionally hardback form.

Initially, in any case, a study of Occultism was perhaps still a little outside my comfort zone and most of my earlier deliveries were on UFO phenomena. A phenomenon which to the uninitiated is as misrepresented as 'little green men' in the same way that ghosts are misidentified as headless horsemen and walled up nuns. Is it not strange, for example, that the alien flying saucer perception of UFOs has only truly existed since the term was coined by a mis-description of Kenneth Arnold's sightings in 1947? Such convex and crescent lights (not saucer shaped according to Arnold at the time) would likely have been regarded as a message from God centuries back.

Just like ghosts and hauntings, ufology also has its 'A' list incidents. America has 'Area 51' and 'Roswell' but in the UK only Rendlesham Forest in Suffolk, seems to be remotely as famous. Interestingly, I was to discover that it was in the direct vicinity of the famous Saxon burial mounds discovered at Sutton Hoo. Perhaps our ancestors thought this place to be rather special as well?

I discovered that Rendlesham has had several UFO sightings, but its fame, of course, came largely from an incident in 1980, where a number of US Air Force personnel claimed to see a UFO, which was reported in a memo to the Ministry of Defence by deputy base commander Lieutenant Colonel Charles I. Halt.

According to the memo, at around 3 a.m. on Boxing Day, a security patrol close to the east gate of the airbase apparently saw lights descending into the forest.

At first, they believed that it was an aircraft crashing, but further investigations led them to an object described in the memo as glowing and metallic in appearance, with coloured lights.

Reportedly, it then began to move through the forest while the animals on a nearby farm apparently went into a frenzy. Subsequently, some of the airmen were to report the flying object landing close to them and further sightings were to be seen in the coming days.

Now, this episode has prompted many books, some of which are now on my shelves, and perhaps the best I have studied so far is *Encounter in Rendlesham Forest* by highly respected author Nick Pope. It has caused much speculation as to what the sightings were, which certainly cannot be summed up in just a few paragraphs. What was far more interesting to me was the fact that after some basic research Rendlesham forest can be seen to be not just a place which had unusual UFO sightings. It is the legendary home of a beast known as a Shug Monkey as well. Eight feet tall, long arms and the face of a snouted monkey like a baboon which has been reported as sighted as late as 2009.

Rendlesham is also a site of poltergeist activity with various reports of stones falling from the sky, in particular, being reported over the years. Add to that the fact that 1980 was perhaps the height of the Cold War to quote an airman from Pope's book: 'After Regan became President, things became very edgy' (p. 46).

I began to wonder if it was possible that people's expectations might be the cause of at least some of the real phenomena.

It is worth also noting that Rendlesham may have been, according to Pope (p. 51–2) a possible site of nuclear weapons at the time. It is likely in any case, when it was used as a military airbase, more conventional equipment would have ensured that a degree of EMF type energies were present.

To quote from an article in the *East Anglia Daily Times* (online) based on the work of researcher Tim Acheson:

In the original Ministry of Defence investigation, the Defence Intelligence staff assessed the levels of radioactivity documented in Lieutenant Colonel Halt's official report as being 'significantly higher than the average background'. (https://www.eadt.co.uk/news/could-radiation-data-help-rendlesham-ufo-case)

In Chapter 15 of Pope's book he notes other prominent incidents recorded by the military. I was fascinated to read about one incident in 1993 described as 'two white lights with a faint red glow at the rear with no engine noise...'

This was reported amongst others by RAF police at an RAF base called Cosford. The very same base where strange things had happened during my first and only investigation with Peter Underwood.

If Rendlesham Forest was a one-off site of apparent phenomena that crossed all spectrums of the paranormal, it would have been of little interest to me. However, as those Amazon deliveries started to pile higher and take up more space than the unused exercise bike, I became convinced that this wasn't the case.

A long forgotten but interesting book took a very different angle for 'crossover' phenomena which took place on Chanctonbury Ring in Sussex. The title of this book was *The Demonic Connection* (Toyne Newton, 1987) which succeeds in making that 'angle' all too clear in its attempt to validate the rumours of a black magic 'sect' in the area at the time.

The ring of trees that surround the top of desolate Chanctonbury Hill has given this place the more mysterious name of Chanctonbury Ring. Whilst the trees were only planted in 1760, its reputation as a place of mystery goes back much further and continues to this day. It was originally used as an Iron Age hill fort and there is evidence that the Romans found the place 'enchanting' enough to build a temple there, possibly to the god Mithras who was eternally at war with evil. Alistair Crowley also found this an equally enchanting place to practise his Magick rituals.

Chanctonbury also has its fair share of legends and hauntings including that of a white bearded Saxon and a meeting with the horned devil if you walk backwards round the ring twelve times.

Perhaps even more interesting than its historical legends is the fact that Chanctonbury also has its share of UFO sightings. This includes one in 1972 where a flickering glow within the trees became a bright red object flying past and brushing the treetops. Other UFO groups were to find very different effects. One group in 1968 experienced temporary loss of their limbs by an unseen force — possibly some similarities to the temporary intense fear and panic I have researched that was sometimes found in The Cage, St Osyth.

I will re-quote the experiences of Kim Sondergaard at The Cage and let the reader decide for themselves their similar nature. 'I began to feel as if my legs would not carry me anymore … I bumped into the wall, into the door and suddenly couldn't stand still.'

In 1974 a group led by the investigator Charles Walker to Chanctonbury was to have one of their participants levitate off the ground — exactly the effect that is supposed to have happened to the teenage girls in the Enfield poltergeist case.

Newton argues that Black Magic rituals may have been taking place in the area. I personally have no idea if this is true or not, but even the rumour might have been enough to trigger that element of stress and panic that often goes with a more conventional paranormal incident.

Let us suppose just for argument's sake that this or other incidents had an element of Magick involved and ask ourselves what this actually entails. In doing so I will refer briefly to the teachings of Alistair Crowley himself. Though we could as easily choose other famous Occultists such as Eliphas Lévi (1810–1875) or Samuel L. Macgregor Mathers (1854–1918), founder of the famous Golden Dawn Occult group.

Crowley's main work, *The Book of the Law*, was apparently written in just three hours through the guiding inspiration of his guardian angel that he called Aiwass. Take away the occultist imagery and this experience is a mirror image of the musical accomplishments of Rosemary Brown dictated to by spirits of those famous dead composers.

Crowley claimed in his autobiography, *The Confessions of Aleister Crowley: An Autohagiography*, ch. 49 that the point of the book was 'the emancipation of mankind from all limitations whatsoever'.

He states in Chapter 3 that 'the technical methods of achieving this are to be studied in [his form of ritual] Magick'.

This lifting of limitations to achieve man's hidden powers seems to me to be like Gurdjieff's 'War on Sleep'. Different rituals, different processes perhaps, but surely different ways to get the same result.

I also discovered that I am by far not the first person to try to join the dots and connect these different categories of paranormal experiences. One of the dearly missed ASSAP 'Old Guard', Hilary Evans, saw obvious similarities between religious experiences of the Virgin Mary by a teenage girl called Delphine and a modern interpretation of a similar teenage girl seeing a spacewoman in her bedroom. In the book *Gods, Spirits and cosmic Guardians* (1987), Evans notes that:

> If I have taken Delphine as a starting point <In my book> it is simply to give myself a fixed point to refer to. In a previous study I took as my starting point .... Glenda who by the age of 12 had been visited by a spacewoman in her bedroom. (p. 10)

I am sure a teenage girl living in between two such cultural points of reference may well have perceived such a thing as being a 'conventional' ghost.

Evans later notes that those who have UFO type (paranormal?) experiences are far more likely to have other types as well. He points out that amongst many others 'Charles Hickson one of the witnesses in the classic 1973 Pascagoula abduction, testified to [differing] anomalous experiences prior to ... abduction'(p. 169).

This is just a small example of Evans' extensive work along these lines.

Another equally fascinating example is the mainly forgotten works of the researcher Albert Budden. Budden also makes that connection between electromagnetic factors (along with other factors) in UFOs and other paranormal experiences. In the well titled book *Electrical UFOs* (1998).

In an interesting paragraph he takes this hypothesis further noting that one of the reported Electromagnetic effects on the consciousness was to evoke subjects to display 'profuse writing ability ... poetry and stream of consciousness/creative compilations are typical' (p. 26). Perhaps this is a way to 'short circuit' extensive rituals which appear to do the same.

By the start of June 2020 as the first lockdown eased, the books were literally falling off my overcrowded shelves. I also felt the obvious need to travel, and what better way to do so than to visit some of the places I had been reading and thinking about in that old Victorian cemetery.

The very first pub I ventured into after this lockdown ended was not in Croydon but the Frankland Arms in Washington. Not Washington DC but the strange remote village of Washington in Sussex, which undoubtedly has historical connections with its vastly bigger brother. It also lies right on the foot of Chanctonbury Hill where I planned to stay the night and savour the stuff of legends, much as I had done in Sandwood Bay about three decades earlier.

The walk itself was splendid and desolate and the view from the top as the sun started to set was truly mystifying. Could I possibly resist walking twelve times backwards around the rings as legend states to 'summon up the horned Devil' or just to see if ritual magic has some effect at all. Harry Price had tried similar; when in the mysterious Hertz Mountains of Germany he once followed an ancient ritual inspired by the poet Goethe to turn an 'innocent' goat into a 'youth of unsurpassing beauty'. If Price could try it, where is the harm in that?

Price, of course, had failed; the goat remained, but a goat 'of some celebrity'. Yet by the second time I walked round the hill, I heard a loud snort behind me and turned and saw a great big horned beast.

Not (perhaps?) the devil — but my way was being blocked by the most exotic rare breed of cattle I had ever seen before with horns, I'd say, at least one foot in length!

An exquisite bit of synchronicity (meaningful coincidence), of which even Carl Jung, the inventor of the term would have hopefully been proud!

As for staying the night, a large group of post-lockdown campers suddenly arrived and broke the magic of the place, so at midnight I returned to my accommodation in Washington, partially thwarted but feeling totally 'free'.

I later travelled to Rendlesham forest which sadly has changed a lot since the famous incident of 1980. The famous UK hurricane of 1987 has changed its nature greatly. The lighthouse at Orford Ness nearby, which was once a possible rational theory for what the airman might have seen, was being demolished during my visit. There is a signed UFO walk through the forest, though my colleagues better versed in the case tell me that the artificial metal UFO structure has been built in the wrong place. What is correct is that Rendlesham has become a slightly amusing UFO 'theme park' and the airbase and any possible electromagnetic effects have long gone in our post-Cold War times.

There were parts of the forest that were still very desolate, atmospheric, and devoid of other people, and I could well imagine at dusk apprehension at the rustle of bushes and the shadow of a Shug Monkey appearing. I was quite startled when I heard a thud behind me which sounding like a stone being thrown or dropped in the moss by an unseen hand. On closer inspection it turned out be a pinecone falling from a great height from a pine tree, and I wondered if this could have been misinterpreted by those who reported the stone throwing poltergeist in the dark of night. A good paranormal perspective, after all, involves first trying to rationalise within our current science.

In this chapter I have mentioned two amusingly strange coincidences that happened to me in the run up and during that strange surreal lockdown. Coincidences happen quite a lot when I am in deep concentration such as when I am writing, more often when I am travelling and 'wide awake' and positive. Whilst I sometimes claim to be as 'psychic as a brick', I sometimes wonder if that is totally true or not.

I will fully admit I only speed read The *Book of the Law* by Crowley — that brand of paranormal called Occultism, I will largely keep for another day. However, I do remember from the lecture that much of what Crowley said is taken out of context. The most famous quote from the book 'Do what thou wilt' is often seen by itself as a licence for excess by the 'Wickedest Man in the World'. Shortly after, there is a far better quote that sums up our, and perhaps his, paranormal quest much better: 'Every man and every woman is a star.'

Perhaps when it comes to paranormal powers, we all must find our own way of getting that 'star' within us to shine bright?

Chapter 7

Two Cases that Recently Came to Light
(Discovering if the real world reflects
the world of ideas)

Little did I realise during my summer excursions of 2020 that a far longer lockdown was going to hit the United Kingdom towards the end of the autumn. Officially there were two lockdowns over that period, a short one during November and an extended one from the end of December to late spring 2021. By then there were so many sub-restrictions grouped in different tiers in different regions that it was impossible to really tell the difference. The regulations supported by the scientific establishment meant it was 'safe' in some regions to eat a substantial meal in bars, but not to drink without a meal. So the country ended up in ridiculous arguments as to whether eating a scotch egg was a meal and therefore gave you COVID-19 immunity.

In the same way as the paranormal community appears to have set aside the thoughts of the likes of Hilary Evens and Albert Budden, whose books had 'appeared' at my door earlier that year, science had forgotten all previous pandemics and appeared to be re-inventing the wheel with random measures. Of particular importance was the 'forgetting' of the fact that all pandemics in recent history (particularly the Spanish flu) had worked through in natural waves. Sweden had the same waves as the UK but with far fewer restrictions. A rational discourse on this can be found from the epidemiologist Abram L. Wagner in his online article 'What Makes a Wave of Disease? An Epidemiologist Explains' (www.theconversation.com/what-makes-a-wave-of-disease-an-epidemiologist-explains).

What this meant, in effect, was that the 'strange art of science' put all of our lives into suspended animation again, quite likely when at the peak of a wave that was about to diminish. My life consisted of online work, reading further books and walks to that strange place called Queens Road Cemetery, which was even stranger when covered with snow in the winter.

Whilst the last remnant of lockdowns was brushed aside in August 2021, getting back to 'normal' has not been an event but a slow process with even the SPR largely still holding all their events online. Under such conditions the possibility of new potentially cutting-edge investigations are thankfully now only just starting to emerge. The new cases I am about to discuss therefore are only new to the extent that they are fairly new to me and not yet reported publicly. I also thought it would be a good way to look into a small number of cases in more detail to see how well they connected with the trends and hypotheses I felt were beginning to emerge.

The second case which I shall discuss in more detail seems in some places to make connections to what might have been previously regarded as old romantic myths. However, you can never cast aside the possibility that such myths do have a basis in fact.

In my book on poltergeists, I gave an example of just such a myth that was local to me but had spread worldwide on YouTube and by way of a small budget movie. This is the case I referred to as the Thornton Heath Poltergeist (early 1970s). I had stated that 'there was just the slimmest of chances that it might be based on some kind of fact' (*Poltergeist*, p. 222).

Yet after its publication, my colleague Alan Murdie conducted some research and did indeed find an initial source. This being a lesser-known book called *The Haunted South* by Joan Forman (1978). Accounts in *The Haunted South* appear to be nearly identical to accounts on which subsequent online publications seem to be based. We will never know how accurate the report of Ms Forman was, but it did show to my surprise that I had literally discarded the fact that this case, at the very least, had a first source. I do, of course, whole heartedly apologise to any YouTubers and others for my initial doubts.

Village Stone Throwing Poltergeist (Early 1970s)

Darren Ritson in his latest book on poltergeists, *Poltergeist Parallels and Contagion* (2021, p. 162), makes an interesting analysis of nine cases that he has thoroughly researched. These are the poltergeist cases at Enfield, (yes, that Enfield case), South Shields, Jarrow, Ashington, Newcastle, Blyth, Gosforth, Howdon, and West Boldon. He looks for parallels in phenomena and discovers, interestingly, to back up my previous thoughts that five of the nine come complete with apparitions.

This is a very useful contribution, though I might argue on some categories that I would not have sub-divided so much.

He notes, for example, that two out of the nine cases involved a fascination with plastic building blocks, and that the same two cases separately involved the throwing of stones. I would perhaps argue that in Denmark (where there is a national obsession for the Lego Building Blocks which they invented) the case ratio there for Lego blocks being thrown would be likely higher. However, as most of these poltergeists were in built-up areas, there would be limitations on any paranormal energy to gather and throw more traditional things such as stones.

In short, it is possible that poltergeists' energy seems to play with or throw whatever it is convenient to get hold of, and stone throwing poltergeists seem to be a product of the countryside. Guy Playfair's research showed them to be very prevalent in some remoter areas of Brazil.

I was therefore particularly interested to get a communication from a lady that we will refer to as 'Mary' through the SPR, who wanted to put on record an ongoing series of stone throwing incidents that had made quite an impact on her earlier life.

After exchanging emails with Mary, I further understood that she simply wanted to make sense of the events in her own mind which had happened at regular intervals over a period of decades. They had started when she was seven in the early 1970s and had continued, all be it in a diminishing way to the turn of the new millennium. The phenomena had primarily consisted of a continual barrage of stones being thrown at the family home, in a small English village. Obviously, a rather malicious prankster could not be initially discounted.

The initial time of contact was in spring 2021, just at the point when restrictions had started to lift but I quickly realised that a visit to the premises (a mid-nineteenth-century house) would only be of limited interest. Normally even without current phenomena the 'lie of the land' can be important in looking for clues. In this case, however, the large garden, from behind which many of the stones had emerged, had drastically changed due to the building of new houses on part of the land. What was also of interest was the fact that a covered stream ran past the property, by now my near first question was to ask if there was a nearby source of water.

I agreed to interview Mary over what turned out to be a long and friendly telephone call. This I followed up with further clarifications. I discovered from my call and subsequent emails that the phenomena could possibly have been triggered following a dispute that Mary's parents had with a mother in a neighbouring house.

The first stones to hit Mary's home smashed through the outer panes of glass in the kitchen window. It started with just one stone per night, but gradually increased until all the back windows were broken. Mary's father replaced them, put up chicken wire to protect them and contacted the police.

Mary was clear that nearly all the events gravitated towards her mother, who she believed to be suffering from stress following the argument and other issues. Her mother could even request a stone to be thrown but with the increasing police watch, it was apparently clear she was not actually throwing the stones. Their doorbell would also sometimes ring spontaneously, which happened once with a policeman inside the house and another outside, within full view of the front door. The police on their frequent visits were often greeted with a stone flying towards their car on arrival. This gave the impression that someone or something was nearly always watching the house. Mary's mother would sometimes faint during the phenomena and on one occasion, after fainting, made strange incomprehensible noises in a male-like voice.

It got to the point where the phenomena could happen nightly for months at a time. As the windows were now protected by mesh, the stones were instead aimed at the main roof to bounce harmlessly down to the flat kitchen roof below. Mary stated that sometimes only one stone would be thrown a day, but sometimes up to one hundred, and if picked up quickly enough were warm to the touch.

Apart from the stones, strange one-off incidents occurred, including finding her father's car though locked in the garage, outside it the next day. More disconcerting would have been the occasion when after returning from a trip, items were arranged in the shape of a cross or swastika, or the time all the chicken wire on the windows was also cut into a swastika shape. This was done so neatly that Mary believed it would have needed some kind of template.

Military personnel from a local base apparently also assisted the ongoing investigation. They tried to aim accurately with a high-powered catapult from possible places where the stones may have emerged from. This apparently had little success when compared with the accuracy of the stones from the mysterious source. Nor could they find the source from using night vision equipment, with the stones appearing in view in flight but their origin remaining unseen.

Not all attempts to help were, in my opinion, constructive. Mary remembers how two paranormal investigators visited the property and made the 'helpful' suggestion that there was a buried well halfway down the garden, complete with the remains of a little boy who had drowned. He was apparently throwing the stones to get some attention. Let us perhaps be thankful that they did not detect a 'portal' to hell behind the garden shed!

Of far more interest to me was the short spate of apparitions that seemed to occur when Mary was still a child. I am, as I have made clear in this book, becoming more aware that apparitions seemed to be identified as archetypes. One of the most famous apparitional archetypes is that of religious people, the young lady referred to by Hilary Evans in a previous chapter saw the Virgin Mary. In the well-known poltergeist case in a council house at East Street, Pontefract, the apparition seen was identified as being that of a hooded monk; despite the house being on a modern development well away from the sites of former monasteries in the historical town.

In our current case the apparent archetype had the elements suggested above. It was also portrayed as harmless, benign and calming — perhaps the ideal apparition for a young female child to see. A **Pink Monk** appeared to on the flat roof of the kitchen to be seen at night by Mary through her bedroom window, this was later seen by her younger sisters as well.

The phenomena very gradually died down, but Mary believes the last stone may have appeared as late as 2001.

What can we make of this very strange series of events?

1. Of course, Mary was initially a young child at the start of the reported phenomena, which does lay open the possibility of misremembering some incidents. This was not always the case though due to the phenomena's longevity. The bare bones of the phenomena were reported in the press at the time giving a good independent source. The Reverend of the diocese during

this period has also contacted me to confirm he was fully aware of the reported phenomena and tried to provide non-interventionalist help. So something strange did indeed apparently occur.

2. A hypothesis of fraud would have likely involved Mary's mother and at least one outsider helping over the duration of more than 20 years. The 'pranksters' would have had to have been skilled enough to avoid detection by police. Taken at face value, at least, this would have required a 'superhuman' effort, which starts to sound just as strange as a 'supernatural' one.

The case seems to tick nearly every factor previously discussed from stress being involved, to a nearby source of water, to the stones being warm.

This type of 'one trick' poltergeist is in no way unique. I mentioned one case in my book on poltergeists; that of the rock throwing poltergeist of Tucson, USA, which behaved in a similar way, but for a lesser duration of time. An Australian colleague of mine in the SPR, Paul Cropper, takes a particular interest in such cases, and has even sourced a report from the Manica Post of Zimbabwe where similar incidents took place in the remote Mutare District close to the Mozambique border.

Here the Chikukwa family reported that family members were being pelted by stones, while invisible beings were biting, pinching, and assaulting them. The stones had followed the children to school and even a small fire had started on their clothes (news.pindula.co.zw/2022/05/07/stones-follow-children-to-school/ 7 May 2022).

There are a few incidents that test a simple 'power within us' theory, or at least put it on a whole new level. The most notable being a car teleporting from within a garage to outside it.

However, overall, I would say that this intriguing case fitted my emerging hypothesis quite well.

Enfield Chase, Camlet Moat, and Cockfosters Cluster

Most of the research done on this case was done by a professional gentleman who has taken an interest in the paranormal for reasons that will become obvious. He also wishes to put his research and experiences on the record. I will refer to the gentleman as 'David' although the places themselves are, of course, fully identifiable.

Enfield Chase is a former Royal Hunting ground in the historical county of Middlesex. Middlesex itself has been incorporated into outer London and does not truly exist in a formal way now other than as having a competitive first-class cricket team. Whilst much of Enfield Chase has been deforested and built over and is more commonly known as the modern suburb of Cockfosters, some parts still have an air of remoteness and mystique. This is particularly true at the northern end of Trent County Park, in which you will find a very strange spot by the name of Camlet Mote.

David is a resident in this area, so in the same way as I have extensively researched my suburb called Croydon, South London (as discussed in my book on poltergeists), he has done a great deal of research in his local area. I envy his in some ways as this local area also includes Green St Enfield, which happens, of course, to be the site of the most famous Enfield Poltergeist of all.

Whilst most historical places have their fair share of ghosts, David was most intrigued to find a particular stretch of road that seemed to have far more than its share. This was a stretch of road from Camlet Way in Barnet through to its intersection with The Ridgeway in Enfield and passing through Beech Hill, Fernery Hill, and Hadley Road in between. Although today it is named as four different roads, it was clear from a map that David sourced dating back to 1757 that these once consisted of a single track through the deep forests of Enfield Chase. With evidence of buildings dating back to the twelfth century, it seemed this stretch of track was certainly much older than that.

At the start of the ancient track there is the ancient village of Monken Hadley which in itself has had a reputation for being a hot spot for inexplicable phenomena. Some would claim it to be the most haunted village in England.

On the edge of Monken Hadley, on Camlet Way, there is Mount House School an old Georgian Mansion likely on the site of an older building. The phenomenon here included the rattle of cartwheels without the presence of carts. This happens, strangely, near the site of two 'Earth Mounds' or 'Mounts' after which the house was named. Whilst the mounds have not been properly excavated, if indeed this location has a special 'resonance', it is possible that the builders of these earth mounds were aware of it as well. Equally intriguing was that a frequent visitor in Victorian times was the author Lord Bulwer Lytton. Lytton happened to be a leading disciple of the famous French occultist Eliphas Levi.

In addition to the very strange 'Mount House', other paranormal places on this stretch of road include a recently active poltergeist at Church House in the 1990s; a blue lady at the former site of the priory; a grey lady or nun at Beacon House; and the ghost of Geoffrey de Mandeville has been seen on Hadley Common.

In this final of just a few examples I should point out that whilst Geoffrey de Mandeville, a twelfth-century knight, is associated with the area, no entity said, 'Hello, my name is Geoffrey'! It is just as likely that any sighting would have been either an archetype or at least a long dead soldier from the medieval Battle of Barnet that took place nearby. This was my point at the start of the chapter in relation to urban legends. They are sometimes just pure legends but at other times can be a colourful way of making sense of real-life incidents.

This old route itself has more than simply its fair share of traditional ghosts. Close to Hadley Woods, and, interestingly, by a small stream, a huge luminous ball up to 10 feet across hovered in front of witnesses in the late 1940s. Such an event these days would likely be recorded as a UFO. A misty white swirling column has also been seen on Camlet Road itself.

The sightings here are historical but get more credence from the fact that further down on Hadley Road, David is aware of an acquaintance who spotted a glowing misty light in front of the windscreen of her car in the mid-1990s. This was also seen by her husband as well.

Such is the reputation of this area that Lord Bulwer Lytton was not the only 'magician' to take an interest in it. My old 'associate' David Farrant unfortunately got fined £10 for trying to raise the spirit of a pirate in Monken Hadley cemetery. Apparently, this was illegal under the little used Ecclesiastical Courts Jurisdiction Act of 1860.

Just off the centre point of this stretch of road is a very strange place indeed known as Camlet Moat. A place of legends and mystery either real, or imagined, or possibly even 'conjured' up within us because this whole area seems so 'special'. Camlet Moat is a scheduled ancient monument consisting of a moat and a space of land covered with undergrowth, trees and with a surprisingly eerie silence. However, to quote from the website of Trent Country Park of which Camlet Moat lies within: 'Nothing is known of the origins of Camlet Moat.'

This makes it a place of wild speculation which can trigger the imagination. It has been known to be a site where magical rituals take place. Pentagrams have been found on the trees and rings of candles in nearby woods. On my own visit there I was greeted by the Four of Hearts and Queen of Spades deliberately left as a tribute to someone or something? If anyone knows any significance that they have, please do feel free to advise me.

What is known about Camlet Moat is that it appeared in local records in 1440 AD and the very limited remains of the drawbridge across the moat were dated to 1357. This timeline makes the romantic legend of the haunting of (the very busy ghost of) Geoffrey De Mandeville at Camlet Moat, as well as on Hadley Common, most unlikely. De Mandeville lived in the twelfth century and actually met his death at Burwell Castle in Cambridgeshire. It is also thought likely that this Camlet Mote was demolished in 1429 and the materials sold to help pay for repairs to Hertford Castle.

There is folklore and half facts which claim this place is in fact Camelot not Camlet the legendary home of the equally legendary King Arthur. This justification, for me, seems tenuous. Perhaps it is the case of a place evoking special feelings simply provoking a myth to justify them. Perhaps that is the essence of many urban legends.

This is just a short selection of the list of places on this route that appear to have had inexplicable phenomena. For those who wish to explore the mystique of this fascinating area further, I would recommend reading the interesting book *Geoffrey De Mandeville and London's Camelot* (1997) by local historian Jennie Lee Cobban.

David's report on this cluster of phenomena was, of course very interesting, but all the more so when he revealed the partial reason he had researched the matter in detail. This was because of a visit he had paid to the local bar/restaurant of the Royal Chace Hotel, just a few hundred metres off Hadley Road. Despite its royal title, the hotel was built according to most sources in 1970, though may well have been built on an older building based on the local maps that David discovered later.

David visited the Royal Chace in August 1994 as the designated driver of a small group of drinkers, so there is little doubt he had his full faculties about him. He cannot fully recollect why he also decided to wear a necklace of haematite that night, a form of iron ore that is reputed to have protective qualities.

Part of the way through the evening David visited the restroom. Nothing unusual in that, except when on venturing into the restroom alone he was faced first by disconcerting noises and then the form of what can only be described as a man dressed in a long shapeless coat of no particular time period. He felt that whatever was facing him was in some way malevolent and was then faced by two much smaller squat nearly square-shaped humanoid creatures. Overall, the whole experience he believes lasted about two minutes.

He regarded the smaller creatures as in some way protective, as not being human type ghosts or sprits but far more likely to be something non-human such as a 'goblin' or a 'boggart'. This an old-fashioned term for a shape shifting mischief making spirit which, when it does appear, tends to do so as a 'a squat hairy man, strong as a six-year-old horse and with arms almost as long as tackle poles', according to the account on Boggarts given by T. Sternberg in his book *Dialect and Folklore of Northamptonshire* (1851).

This quote from Sternberg roughly encapsulates David's later drawings of the 'humanoid' beings after the incident. Strangely, about a mile away there is an area that used to be referred to as Bull Boggarts Hollow, which shows that such 'categorising' of a paranormal event had likely been quite common nearby, in the past.

I have since asked David about any other paranormal experiences he has had, and he has explained to me that he has experienced various things since the age of three including telepathy, precognition of future events and UFO sightings. I can't help wondering if he would be one of the small percentages of people easily susceptible to conjuring up special powers in deep trance hypnotism. Perhaps I might discuss that with him at some point.

Assuming David's and Mary's experiences are truly paranormal in nature; I keep coming back to the same question. Is it possible or even plausible that people like David are a magnet for alien beings, boggarts, and long dead 'seers' who whisper future events into his ear? Or is it far more likely that all these phenomena are one and the same. Could it be that there is ONE power that conveys itself as a Pink Monk to a child, that alternatively conveys itself as a UFO, when that power is evoked near an airbase, and a Goblin or Boggart when spotted within the magical historical outer region of London that once was Enfield Chase?

Put like that the 'One Paranormal Power' solution seems so obvious. After all, since learning about 'infinity', when tracing my finger around the line of a tennis ball as a young child, I think I always liked the bigger and simpler ideas. This surely seems to be backed up by the way that science works.

Perhaps, though, I shouldn't forget that this is a book on *my own* paranormal perspective! It's my book with my experiences and I can, in fact, put things exactly as I want. As a writer I can, in effect, create my own truth. I can downgrade characters and incidents I don't agree with and behave like the emperor of my own little written world. A bit like the 'little emperor syndrome' of an infant, who knows little about reality, beyond dreaming and tracing his finger round that damned tennis ball.

Or to put it more simply:

Can one person's personal reflections on a complex subject that has been fascinating people for years, possibly hope to achieve in some way an overall theory?

Chapter 8

On the Eighth Day!
(Does the idea of 'One Big Paranormal Box' provide inspiration or more frustration in the quest for paranormal truth?)

An idea, like a ghost, must be spoken to a little before it will explain itself.

(Charles Dickens)

In the Kabbalistic teachings of Jewish mysticism, the number seven is a symbol of perfection, or at least the perfection that can be created by natural means. The natural world was created in seven days. There are also seven colours in a rainbow which symbolises hope and beauty after a storm (and in other traditions, a pot of gold for the even luckier few).

The number eight, however, symbolises something quite different. It is symbolic of an entity or power that is beyond the natural order of things. Kabbalistic teachings would call this the mysterious 'Ein Sof' (the infinite), whilst Christians and others would simply call this God. Sceptics such as Richard Dawkins might refer to this as non-existent superstitious nonsense.

Whatever your views on the subject, a book such as this certainly needs its eighth and final chapter.

As 2022 started there was perhaps a flicker of that rainbow of hope as well. In the UK, after much debate, we avoided further lockdowns and the cancelling of a second Christmas. The serious threat of COVID-19 is now discussed in more proportional ways, so it very much seems to be a start of a brand new 'week' in all our lives.

Christmas was spent in a rented studio on the fringes of what is the delightful but most misnamed National Park in the whole of the UK — that of the 'New Forest'. This forest was 'new' in 1086 when it was proclaimed a *Nova Foresta* or new royal hunting forest by William the Conqueror. It was perhaps most extensively used in the thirteenth century by the tyrannical King John who visited his hunting lodge in nearby Ramsey in between more mythical visits to Shere on the search for bathing maidens in the now 'haunted' Silent Pool!

In any case, the New Forest is a beautiful place and a next to normal Christmas was finally had.

In February 2022 I received an email from the enthusiastic and engaging Marketing and Publicity Manager of my current publisher, 6th Books, with an idea to include me in a series of books exploring the paranormal journeys of various people from various angles. This series of books had a working title of *Paranormal Perspectives*. My initial thought was to hesitate, after all, I had been in partial lockdown since my last book with some limitations on investigations and research. I also thought an autobiography style in such a specialised field would be 'presumptuous' and a little pompous. The only examples to date, I believe, are Harry Price, *The Search for Truth* (1942) who some will claim contains a few 'untruths' as well, and a perfectly passable effort by Peter Underwood, *No Common Task* (1983). The fact is that this style, at least in the UK has not been attempted for nearly 40 years for a book on investigating the paranormal.

I conveyed these initial doubts to 6th books, but the Marketing and Publicity Manager is a persuasive as well as an engaging kind of guy. The more I thought about possible approaches, the more I became fascinated with doing a short 'meditation' on the subject itself based around key events in my paranormal (and occasionally 'normal') life. Robert Pirsig did an excellent job when doing the same in a much longer book about metaphysics in *Zen and the Art of Motorcycle Maintenance*. The very least I could do is give it a damned good try!

I tend to write best in the afternoon and evening when the caffeine effects from the 'Nespresso' machine (that I didn't put back in the attic) have fully kicked in. This can be supplemented by the occasional 'vape' of nicotine with flavours I only recently learnt existed. When I get to that optimum writing state, I find that my mind starts to look for 'connections'. Some are simply 'amusing' light touch narrative connections that I hope improve the flow of the narrative. These would include the reintroduction of that 'Nespresso' machine in this chapter which I wrote about as so important in lockdown, and briefly bringing 'King John' back into the narrative earlier as well.

There is also a second type of connection that maybe has some relevance such as discovering that the successful investigation I had with Peter Underwood at RAF Cosford discussed in Chapter Two was also the sight of a major UFO sighting as well (Chapter 6). In such a case I let the reader decide if the connection is there.

When I write in this very alert state, I also find I am 'discovering' in my own head at least far more profound connections, that I hope are minor 'Eureka! — I have found it!' moments. A term reputed to have been coined by the famous ancient Greek mathematician Archimedes when his body made his bath overflow and he started to understand the mathematical concept of displacement. This type of connection would include such things as finding examples of profound similarity between UFO encounters and more traditional apparitions and paranormal activity. In effect, the essence of my personal paranormal quest so far.

At the end of the last chapter, I started to raise some doubts as to how far I could take this 'One Big Paranormal Box' narrative based solely on my own interpretation of events. Somewhere in this process I decided that we do need to look much more closely as to how the mind comes to such 'connections' that cause such 'Eureka' moments.

Most of us who study the paranormal are aware of the effect of pareidolia when the brain instinctively makes sense of a random image, when a shadow in the attic becomes a ghostly nun or monk. Could it not also be the case that 'pareidolia' or its equivalent can also affect the mind directly and make 'connections' when the facts are random?

For the crystallisation of that particular thought, I would have to in particular thank Nick Pope for a passage he wrote in his excellent book *Encounter in Rendlesham Forest*, in which he refers to this process of seeking connections as 'like assembling a jigsaw puzzle with the picture only becoming clear when enough small pieces have been assembled' (p. 44).

But Pope goes on to warn against seeing connections that simply aren't there and points out that sometimes:

Because of an analyst's personal view or perception, a conclusion-led approach is taken. A good example would be the way in which certain people went looking for a connection between the 9/11 terror attacks and Saddam Hussein's regime, because that's what they expected (and in some cases wanted) to find. (p. 44)

If I transfer this excellent logic to the current issue in hand, I would then be faced with the following question.

Could my own thinking process write a meditation on my own paranormal life, already aiming to show the likelihood of the paranormal, without automatically finding such possibly tenuous 'connections'?

If we were, indeed, dealing with a brand-new theory, such connections would make the conclusions 'wishful' at best. However, whilst my narrative might have developed this theory gradually, in the same way that I acquired it gradually during my experiences of the paranormal, the theory itself has been formed and reformed many times in slightly different ways. It has never been falsified but has far too often simply been put to one side, as we seem to prefer the misunderstood romance of ad hoc compartmentalisation.

My colleague in the Ghost Club, Dr Robert Radaković, has written a fascinating PhD about the belief and motivations of those in the forefront of what has become modern paranormal research called 'Beyond Faith and Reason: The Genesis of Psychical Research and the Search for the Paranormal Domain (1850–1914)'. It becomes clear from this study and other studies as well that this lazy compartmentalisation was not our starting point.

One of Radaković's key arguments is that this new study of the paranormal:

> Necessitated a new intellectual methodology, with some choosing to investigate unusual paranormal phenomena, a tertium quid approach which considered aspects of philosophy, science, and religion in combination.... (p. 9)

Tertium Quid means a third thing that is undefined but is related to two definite or known things. This seems to encapsulate a search for one missing element. What, in fact, the writer Colin Wilson has previously referred to as the missing Faculty X.

Many of the early highly scholarly participants in our subject seemed to share this view as well.

Sir Oliver Lodge (1851–1940), who arguably invented modern radio, (in between being an active member of both the SPR and the Ghost Club), according to Radaković 'conveyed a belief in a universal interconnectedness, or One Truth' (p. 67).

While William Crookes (1832–1919), a chemist who was a key factor in the invention of vacuum tubes (while also having time to join the SPR, the Ghost Club, and the important occult society the Hermetic Order of the Golden Dawn):

Posited the existence of a general paranormal faculty which he called a Psychic Force ... [which] whatever it was, acted in a capricious manner, and that this unpredictability should be taken into account during investigations. (p. 124)

I wish I had thought of the word 'capricious' earlier, it sums up what we are up against nicely with regard to the paranormal.

Radaković also points out that even the out and out spiritualists of this time 'regarded orthodox science as merely a subset of their own "new science", and thus inadequate to explain all the intricacies of the universe' (p. 68).

This means like me they were searching for a new scientific paradigm. Whether their paradigm was right or wrong is not the current point.

This search for an overall paranormal theory has come and gone and come back again over the years. It perhaps most significantly was reinvigorated with the multi-disciplinary approach that came with the founding of ASSAP in 1981, and the work which I have mentioned earlier of Hilary Evans and Hugh Pincott amongst many others. One of the most prominent 'others' would be the writer and researcher Paul Devereaux, with his breakthrough work *Earthlights* (1982). This is an excellent effort to look for correlations between UFO type experiences and natural geological faults whose energy could just be the trigger. He also looks at the distribution of standing stones and ancient sites of potential sacred interest in the UK and compares them with the distribution of such geological faults. The maps he produced appear to the naked eye to show that our ancestors were a little less compartmentalised than us. They were simply aware that certain areas were in some way special — places worthy of 'worship' and places potentially containing a 'box' of 'magical' powers. I am unsure these days whether the maps he produced could be put through any twenty-first-century computer analysis to prove these correlations, which appear to go far beyond any case of 'intellectual' pareidolia.

Devereux states that:

> The UFO is a profoundly sensitive energy form. Practical magicians develop their PK expertise by concentrating on a candle flame, as this is matter in a particularly tenuous state susceptible to subtle influences. The UFO form is a 'very wonderful fire'. (ch. 8, p. 216)

This concept of 'oneness' in the paranormal, is not too dissimilar to the debates about one God or many (theism vs. polytheism). Richard Swinburne is a great believer in the former and can, I think, win this argument logically by defining a god as omnipotent (all powerful) leaving little room for God number two, three, or four. Whilst at the start of the book I made a close analogy with the God, no God debate, once the concept of an absolute power is discarded, we can only look to empirical evidence, not logic, to prove that a special (but not quite omnipotent/godlike) paranormal power exists.

I can say that over the last few decades there is evidence that these connections and correlations point towards one 'box' of paranormal powers. What is certainly true is that others in the past have seen such connections as well. The more people who see that the picture in the jigsaw is the same, the less likely it is that the pieces have been put together incorrectly, at least.

If I had achieved some connexions and correlation, had I also achieved cause in this theory?

There are also some types of paranormal that wouldn't sit so comfortably within a new 'hidden power within us' theory. The key ones would perhaps be those which challenged our whole notion of space and time and include those paranormal events which relate to time slips and precognition. Time may be 'relative' according to Einstein but time travel whether in the mind or the body would possibly take one hell of a quantum leap beyond his own quantum physics.

Of course, the three main issues with showing premonitions to be true are

1. being able to decipher what they are, in fact, a premonition of;
2. being able to in some way put them on record before the event; and
3. being able to decide if the information could have been gathered in natural ways or even supernatural ways not involving direct knowledge of the future.

With regard to point number one, does this famous quote from the seer Nostradamus really predict the great fire of London as many believe?

The blood of the just will commit a fault at London,
Burnt through lightning of twenty threes the six:
The ancient lady will fall from her high place,
Several of the same sect will be killed.

In which case who was the ancient lady and does a fire in a bakery (the reported cause) really stand up to the 'lightning' test?

Point number two is quite problematic as well. Perhaps the most extensive case of precognitions of modern disasters came from the Aberfan tragedy when in 1964 a huge mountain of coal collapsed onto a school in Aberfan, Wales. This killed 144 people, 116 of whom were children. John Barker, a psychologist in a nearby town was intrigued as to whether this event had been predicted and persuaded the *London Evening Standard* newspaper to run an article on the subject. He received 76 responses, 36 of which were received in dreams, some impressive, but all by definition recorded after the event.

Barker perhaps realised this weakness in post-event testimony and set up a premonitions' bureau. The responses were mixed: some accurate ones and many wide of the mark. This project was to have a 'romantically' spine chilling ending after Barker died of a brain tumour. When his records were searched, a memo was found with two accurate predictions of his death.

With regard to point number three, when is precognition actually a journey into the future? When you think of a friend and he suddenly rings, did your mind go into the future and tell you that call was coming, or did you perhaps tune into your friend's need to call you in a far easier to (scientifically) explain form of ESP. In my book on poltergeists, I make use of a quote from Colin Wilson, which makes this point even better. This quote concerns the hunter James Corbett who had inexplicably changed his walking route and the next day found when retracting his footsteps that 'in the sandy bed of the culvert, [on the route he avoided] on the left-hand side, he discovered the pug marks of a tiger that had been lying there' (*Poltergeist*, p. 195).

Was it precognition or the mind in a heighted state tuning in to life-threatening danger? Similar could also be said for cases that involve apparent time slips. The most famous case perhaps being the experiences of two ladies, Charlotte Anne Moberly and Eleanor Jourdain, who in 1901 visited the Palace of Versailles in France and believed they had entered the time of Marie Antoinette c. 1789. The reasons for their belief included the style of the clothes of others around them, the music that was playing, the style of farming implements as well as other factors.

These were, however, two ladies who from past experiences appeared to be in that special small percentage of people who are more 'psychically' gifted. Is it not easier to look at their experience (which they described as strangely two dimensional) as more akin to a UFO abduction experience? Their contemporary George Tyrell (mathematician, physicist, and SPR parapsychologist) suggested 'this might have been a case of telepathy rather than of retrocognition, the possible agent being one or more of people with knowledge of the events of 1789'.

What I seem to have observed through the cases myself and others have tirelessly investigated is a whole host of factors that appear to trigger all types of the paranormal. These would include personal state of mind factors which are intriguingly but also confusingly from both sides of the spectrum. The presence of stress and anxiety seem to be very important in uncontrolled phenomena such as that caused by a poltergeist but a calm trance-like state seems important for cases where such powers seem to be able to be channelled.

With regard to external factors, these seem to primarily extend to electromagnetic and geomagnetic influences, and also to the presence of water and possibly other natural factors as well. All three may be connected, of course, as water is a good conductor. The mechanisms that cause phenomena are still way beyond my comprehension. Indeed, I would be suspicious of those who claim a full understanding of it as their 'understanding' is likely more akin to their own beliefs.

There is so much still to explain! We do not yet fully comprehend *how* such a 'power' can cause a UFO type ball of light, throw an object across the room, or even interact with the mind of another in ESP. Does that power always need a human agent to cause it or can such incidents happen unseen and unrecorded?

Did you really expect a short book on my paranormal life to definitively prove the cause of the paranormal?

Then I have that not so little issue of how to fit in or not fit in God and the afterlife at all. It seems that whilst my thoughts don't explicitly exclude it they do not rely on it either. Surely an omnipotent god (or for that matter past life spirits) would have no need for electromagnetism or heightened states of consciousness to produce his or her afterlife miracles?

I might not get a 'B+ or possibly better' from Swinburne this time for this conclusion, after all, his logic points to a conventional God. I would hope, at least, he would be open-minded as to how I got there. Perhaps I shall send him a copy of this book just to find out.

In a few weeks at the start of September 2022 I will be giving my first talk on this re-discovered angle to the fortieth birthday conference of ASSAP. It will, in fact, be the first talk I have given face to face since all our lives were sadly interrupted by COVID-19. I am writing notes for this talk in between writing this chapter and have decided it would be quite frankly silly to use it to try to change long-held perfectly genuine views of others.

In between amusing anecdotes, which I never can resist, I will simply be quoting the simplicity of the scientist Kuhn and the natural simplicity of at least opening the mind to the possibility of a 'One Big Box' theory. I will ask the listeners to ask themselves the following things in the work they do in the future.

1. Are different types of phenomena based around the same people who can tune in to its source or act as a catalyst?
2. Are different types of phenomena based around similar places or environments?
3. If the phenomena do not fit the above criteria — is the evidence for it strong and precluding a natural explanation? (This question should, of course, be asked for all types of apparently paranormal phenomena.)

The above points are simple reasonable observations that we should all be making to achieve a 'good' perspective on the paranormal. How reasonable my peers find them, I will discover in time.

A 'good' perspective on life, however, should be more than just judged on any supernatural aspects. Proust's words from Chapter One are true whether the experiences they convey trigger paranormal experiences or not.

You should never leave yourself 'weary after a dull day with the prospect of a depressing morrow'.

Find your own version of that special Madeleine cake and cease to feel 'mediocre, accidental, mortal'.

This is likely the only paranormal book in the infinite universe that makes mention of Peter 'The Cat' Bonetti, and of the writer's own respectable but limited goalkeeping skills. Whilst every event I mentioned is factually correct, it was included as mostly an analogy to following one's dreams whatever they are. If I had followed a different path, it would have been far more likely to have been a political one. It is reasonable to say I could write a whole book on my experiences as a younger man travelling Europe as International Officer of the Young Liberal Democrats. Here, as I mentioned previously several of my peers gained fairly high office in time. As an example, when I was leaving the Liberal Democrat youth wing, a certain young lady called Elizabeth Truss was just beginning her journey there. I believe she later changed party and joined the Conservatives- to become Prime Minister for an 'infinitesimally' short space of time! However, as an analogy to following one's dreams, politics has far less of an instinctive mainstream appeal.

Perhaps then we shouldn't follow Aleister Crowley's suggestion of 'Do what thou wilt' but at the very least we should do our best to 'Do what thou dreams'!

After all, whist the paranormal needs dreamers and thinkers, dreamers and thinkers don't necessarily need the paranormal!

You may prefer the fresh wind on your face from the unique motorbike journey that the 'sceptical' Robert Pirsig took, to the fresh wind through the windowless ruin of that cottage at Sandwood Bay, or the infinite combination of things in between.

So, some of this book is romantic speculation; much I hope is working hypothesis, but the fact that a dreamer needs dreams is the most important theory of the 'science' of life.

It is this final theory, at least, that needs constant 'experimentation' to perfect!

References

Brittle, G. (2002) *The Demonologist: The Extraordinary Career of Ed and Lorraine Warren*. Bloomington, Indiana: iUniverse Books

Budden, A (1998) *Electrical UFOs*. London: Cassell Illustrated

Cobban, J. L. *Geoffrey De Mandeville and London's Camelot Ghosts, Historical Mysteries and the Occult in Barnet*. Barnet, London: Barnet Museum and Local History Society

Crowley, A. *The Confessions of Aleister Crowley: An Autohagiography*. (1989) London: Penguin New Edition

Crowley, A. (1977) *The Book of the Law*. Newburyport, Massachusetts: Red Wheel, New edition

Dawkins, R. (2006) *The God Delusion*. London: Bantam Press

Devereaux, P. (1982) *Earthlights*. London: HarperCollins

Evans, H. (1987) *Gods, Spirits and Cosmic Guardians*. Wellingborough, Northamptonshire: Aquarian Press

Forman, J. (1978) *The Haunted South*. London: Robert Hale Ltd

Fraser, J. (2010) *Ghost Hunting: A Survivor's* Guide. Cheltenham: The History Press

Fraser, J. (2020) *Poltergeist: A New Investigation into Destructive Haunting*. Winchester/Washington: 6th Books

Green, A. (1973) *Ghost Hunting: A Practical Guide*. London: Garnstone Press

Gurdjieff, G. I. (1963) *Meetings with Remarkable Men*. Boston, Massachusetts, E. P. Dutton, and Co Inc

Gurdjieff, G. I. (1950) *Beelzebub's Tales to His Grandson*. New York: Harcourt, Brace and Company

Harper, C. (1907) *Haunted Houses*. London: Chapman & Hall

Henderson, J. A. (2001) *The Ghost That Haunted Itself*. Edinburgh: Mainstream Publishing

Kuhn T. S. (1962) *The Structure of Scientific Revolutions*. Chicago: University of Chicago Press

Manning, M. (1975) *The Link*. New York: Henry Holt and Company Inc.

Newton, T. (1987) *The Demonic Connection*. Poole: Blandford Press

Morris, R. (2006) *Harry Price: The Psychic Detective*. Stroud Gloucestershire: Sutton Publishing Ltd

Pirsig, R. (1974) *Zen and the Art of Motorcycle Maintenance*. New York City: William Morrow and Company

Pope, N. (2015) *Encounter in Rendlesham Forest*. New York City: St. Martin's Griffin

Playfair, G. (1981) *This House Is Haunted*. London: Shere Books

Price H. (1940) *The Most Haunted House in England*. London: Longmans, Green and Co Ltd

Radaković, R. (Thesis, 2019) *Beyond Faith and Reason: The Genesis of Psychical Research and the Search for the Paranormal Domain* (1850–1914). https://eprints.lancs.ac.uk/id/eprint/136241/

Randi, J. (1975) The Magic of Uri Geller. New York City: Ballantine Books, Inc

Ritson, D. (2021) *Poltergeist Parallels and Contagion*. Guildford: White Crow Books

Swinburne, R (1996) *Is There a God?* Oxford: Oxford University Press

Tupper, M. F. (1858) *Stephan Langton or The Days of King John: A Romance of the Silent Pool*. Guildford: Biddles Ltd (21st Edition)

Underwood, P. (1983) *No Common Task*. London: George G. Harrap & Co Ltd

Underwood, P. (1994) *Nights in Haunted Houses*. London: Headline Books

Underwood, Peter (1986) *The Ghost Hunter's Guide*. London: Blandford Press

Warren, J. P. (2009) *How to Hunt Ghosts: A Practical Guide*. New York: Atria Books

Wilson, C. (1971) *The Occult*. New York: Random House

ALL THINGS PARANORMAL

Investigations, explanations and deliberations on the paranormal, supernatural, explainable or unexplainable. 6th Books seeks to give answers while nourishing the soul: whether making use of the scientific model or anecdotal and fun, but always beautifully written.
Titles cover everything within parapsychology: how to, lifestyles, alternative medicine, beliefs, myths and theories.
If you have enjoyed this book, why not tell other readers by posting a review on your preferred book site?

Recent bestsellers from 6th Books are:

The Scars of Eden
Paul Wallis
How do we distinguish between our ancestors' ideas of God
and close encounters of an extraterrestrial kind?
Paperback: 978-1-78904-852-0 ebook: 978-1-78904-853-7

The Afterlife Unveiled
What the dead are telling us about their world!
Stafford Betty
What happens after we die? Spirits speaking through mediums
know, and they want us to know. This book unveils their
world…
Paperback: 978-1-84694-496-3 ebook: 978-1-84694-926-5

Harvest: The True Story of Alien Abduction
G. L. Davies
G. L. Davies's most-terrifying investigation yet reveals one
woman's terrifying ordeal of alien visitation, nightmarish
visions and a prophecy of destruction on a scale never before
seen in Pembrokeshire's peaceful history.
Paperback: 978-1-78904-385-3 ebook: 978-1-78904-386-0

Wisdom from the Spirit World
Carole J. Obley
What can those in spirit teach us about the enduring bond of
love, the immense power of forgiveness, discovering our life's
purpose and finding peace in a frantic world?
Paperback: 978-1-78904-302-0 ebook: 978-1-78904-303-7

Spirit Release
Sue Allen
A guide to psychic attack, curses, witchcraft, spirit attachment, possession, soul retrieval, haunting, deliverance, exorcism and more, as taught at the College of Psychic Studies.
Paperback: 978-1-84694-033-0 ebook: 978-1-84694-651-6

Advanced Psychic Development
Becky Walsh
Learn how to practise as a professional, contemporary spiritual medium.
Paperback: 978-1-84694-062-0 ebook: 978-1-78099-941-8

Where After
Mariel Forde Clarke
A journey that will compel readers to view life after death in a completely different way.
Paperback: 978-1-78904-617-5 ebook: 978-1-78904-618-2

Poltergeist! A New Investigation into Destructive Haunting
John Fraser
Is the Poltergeist "syndrome" the only type of paranormal phenomena that can really be proven?
Paperback: 978-1-78904-397-6 ebook: 978-1-78904-398-3

A Little Bigfoot: On the Hunt in Sumatra
Pat Spain
Pat Spain lost a layer of skin, pulled leeches off his nether
regions, and was violated by an Orangutan for this book
Paperback: 978-1-78904-605-2 ebook: 978-1-78904-606-9

Astral Projection Made Easy
and overcoming the fear of death
Stephanie June Sorrell
From the popular Made Easy series, Astral Projection
Made Easy helps to eliminate the fear of death through
discussion of life beyond the physical body.
Paperback: 978-1-84694-611-0 ebook: 978-1-78099-225-9

Haunted: Horror of Haverfordwest
G. L. Davies
Blissful beginnings for a young couple turn into a nightmare
after purchasing their dream home in Wales in 1989.
Paperback: 978-1-78535-843-2 ebook: 978-1-78535-844-9

Readers of ebooks can buy or view any of these bestsellers by clicking on the live link in the title. Most titles are published in paperback and as an ebook. Paperbacks are available in traditional bookshops. Both print and ebook formats are available online.

Find more titles and sign up to our readers' newsletter at
www.6th-books.com

Join the 6th books Facebook group at
6th Books The world of the Paranormal